MALAYSIA

DIVING GUIDE

Berkeley Books Pte Ltd
Singapore

ENRICHMENT ANSWER KEY
Reading Grade 2

Page 69   Answers will vary, but should indicate the main idea of the picture.

Page 70   Students should be able to pick up the ice cube with the thread.

Page 71   Words will vary, but should belong in the categories.

Page 72   Answers will vary, but should be related to what is shown in the picture.

ENRICHMENT ANSWER KEY
Reading Grade 2

Page 65   Answers will vary.

Page 66   Drawings will vary.

Page 67   baseball, downtown, newspaper, lunchbox, notebook, armchair, sidewalk, sunshine, hilltop, goldfish, backyard, bathtub

m	n	s	u	n	s	h	i	n	e	h
g	o	l	d	f	i	s	h	p	b	i
f	t	m	w	q	r	i	l	y	a	l
p	e	n	l	v	c	d	w	b	t	l
b	b	e	u	v	x	e	m	a	h	t
d	o	w	n	t	o	w	n	s	t	o
z	o	s	c	z	s	a	p	e	u	p
g	k	p	h	i	j	l	t	b	b	x
o	v	a	b	a	c	k	y	a	r	d
k	l	p	o	e	i	u	h	l	j	m
y	m	e	x	b	r	a	y	j	h	z
f	a	r	m	c	h	a	i	r	t	o

Page 68   *Lines between:* is not–isn't, we are–we're, he will–he'll; I will–I'll, have not–haven't, they will–they'll, could not–couldn't, that is–that's, did not–didn't; she is–she's, can not–can't, you are–you're

MALAYSIA
DIVING GUIDE

Texts and photographs
Andrea and Antonella Ferrari

Editorial production
Valeria Manferto De Fabianis
Laura Accomazzo

Graphic design
Patrizia Balocco
Clara Zanotti

Illustrations of the dives
Cristina Franco

Biological files
Text
Angelo Mojetta

Illustrations
Monica Falcone
Lucia Mongioj

Translation
Studio Traduzioni Vecchia

THAILAND

VIETNAM

SOUTH

PENISULAR MALAYSIA

•Kuala Lumpur

SINGAPORE

Contents

CHINA
PACIFIC OCEAN
INDIA
MALAYSIA
INDONESIA
BORNEO
PAPUA NEW GUINEA
INDIAN OCEAN
AUSTRALIA

CHINA SEA

MALAYSIA

Layang Layang

Abdul Rahman National Park

Kota Kinabalu

Labuan Island

BRUNEI

SABAH

SARAWAK

Pulau Mabul and Kapalai

Pulau Sipadan

Kuching

BORNEO

1 This extraordinary photograph shows the strange snout of a blue pufferfish resting on the coral seabed.

2-3 A close-up of a school of barracuda reveals their pointed snouts and silvery scales.

© 1997 White Star S.r.l.
This English edition first published in Singapore, Malaysia & Indonesia in 1997 by Berkeley Books Pte. Ltd., 5 Little Road 08-01 Singapore 536983, by arrangement with White Star S.r.l., Via C. Sassone 24, 13100 Vercelli, Italy.

All rights of translation, reproduction, and partial or total adaptation, by any means whatsoever, are reserved for all nations.

ISBN 962-593-170-8

Printed in Italy by Grafiche Mazzucchelli, MILANO.
In the month of April 1997
Colour separations by Magenta, Lit. Com., SINGAPORE

INTRODUCTION

Malaysia is rapidly becoming to Western visitors what it has been for some time to Asian ones - an extraordinary and accessible diving paradise.
This is not the place to describe the many beautiful and interesting attractions of the Malaysian peninsula and northern Borneo, the two areas which together make up this Southeast Asian country. Tropical latitudes and a warm, humid climate have given it extraordinarily rich flora and fauna, as well as breathtaking natural sights and landscapes. Malaysia's fascinating indigenous tribes are another reason to visit. Here we will concentrate on diving in Malaysia, which is certainly less well-known than it deserves to be, despite the international fame which Sipadan has enjoyed for years.
Indeed, there are many factors which contribute to making the seabeds of Malaysia, especially those in the South China Sea and the Sulawesi Sea, off the coast of Borneo, a destination with few equals in the world and one which

A - The presence of swift currents and vertical walls guarantees the flourishing development of filtering organisms in the Malaysian seas.

B - The top reefs exposed to strong sunlight are teeming vats of biodiversity which increasingly require protection.

C - In the areas in which the reef has not been damaged, many large specimens such as this Tridacna maxima can still be seen.

D - There are numerous large barrel sponges on the deeper, plankton-rich seabeds.

E - The atolls which are more distant from the mainland, such as Layang Layang, are characterised by particularly transparent waters.

F - On the Malaysian seabeds you can admire large concentrations of species, such as this lobster, Palinurus versicolor, which have become rare elsewhere.

A

B

C

the demanding diver cannot afford to miss.
Malaysia's geographical location, in the heart of the Indo-Pacific basin, and thus in the center of the area with the greatest marine biodiversity in the world, puts it on par with Indonesia and Papua New Guinea, which have many more species than the central Pacific Ocean or the Indian Ocean, for example.
Moreover, many diving destinations in Malaysia have advantages over all of these. While classical destinations such as the Caribbean, the Red Sea and the Maldives have become too crowded (if not actually deteriorated in certain points)

because of their development as tourist attractions, most Indonesian sites, with the exception of well-known diver haunts such as Bali and Manado, still fail to operate reliably.
At the other extreme, Papua New Guinea has opted for exclusively elite tourism and charges prohibitive prices, partly because of the difficult environmental conditions with which local operators must contend.
In contrast, several factors combine to make Malaysia an ideal destination for the diver who wants to use his time and money intelligently. These include dynamic private Malaysian companies, the locals'

D

most exacting diver can easily enjoy a range of activities from classical dives in coral gardens at shallow depths (the domain of macrophotography, especially in the diving areas on the Malaysian peninsula, the Tunku Abdul Rahman Park and Mabul, still attached to the continental shelf), to more difficult dives on impressive vertical walls rising directly from the world's deepest abyss, such as at Sipadan or Layang Layang, the haunts of large pelagic predators. Then there is the rare thrill of diving in a pass, in lakes of brackish water and labyrinthine mangrove forests, in search of species which often have not yet

CLIMATE

Encompassing Peninsular Malaysia and the states of Sabah and Sarawak in northern Borneo, Malaysia enjoys a tropical climate influenced by monsoonal winds. During the wet monsoon (from December to March) winds from the northeast prevail, while the dry monsoon (from May to November) is announced by prevailing southwesterly winds. Overall the climate is complex and heavily influences the movement of currents and the operation of individual diving centres. For example, the atoll of Layang Layang is closed to tourists from November to March

E

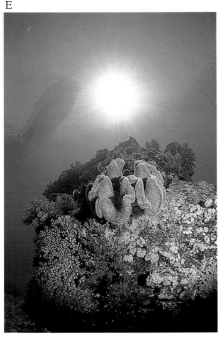

F

traditional flair for trade, a stable economic structure (Malaysia is one of the so-called "Asian Tigers"), punctual and reliable domestic and international connections (the national carrier, Malaysian Airlines, operates regularly, with numerous stops in major European airports), religious and cultural tolerance (the official religion is Islam, but citizens enjoy religious freedom) and the professionalism of the diving centers that operate in the areas discussed in this guide. Added to these factors, of course, are the extraordinary variety of Malaysian seabeds and their stupendous richness of species. With minimum effort even the

been given an official scientific classification.
Essentially, during a properly organized stay of two or three weeks in Malaysia, the diver can admire a quantity and variety of species and environments which are truly unparalleled anywhere else in the world. We hope that this guide to the most beautiful dives in the country will help the reader plan and organize their own exciting voyage.

(during the wet monsoon) due to the high waves and torrential rains that lash the South China Sea and the eastern coast of the Malaysian peninsula (also affecting the islands of Pulau Tioman, Pulau Redang and Pulau Perhentian), while Pulau Mabul, Pulau Sipadan and Sangalaki, protected by the land mass of Borneo, can remain open all year. At any rate, all ocean areas can be expected to be windy, warm and humid, with an occasional night-time thunderstorm as the rainy season approaches. Water temperature varies throughout the year from a minimum of 27°C to a maximum of 31°C.

DANGEROUS ANIMALS

S pecies in the Malaysian waters which are potentially dangerous to humans are basically the same as those in all other tropical and equatorial seas. They are creatures which may attack in order to eat, defend their territory or survive.

We should note several species of shark (especially the silvertip shark *Carcharhinus albimarginatus*, the grey reef shark *Carcharhinus amblyrhynchos*, the scalloped hammerhead shark *Sphyrna lewini*, the whitetip reef shark *Triaenodon obesus*, and the oceanic whitetip shark *Carcharhinus longimanus*), all magnificent and imposing creatures which under normal conditions are timid, cautious and quite difficult to approach, as any diver with a degree of experience can attest. There is always the chance of a nocturnal encounter

C

D

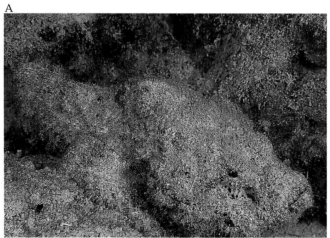

A

B

A - Almost all members of the Scorpaenidae *family are distinguished by their impressive mimetic abilities. Here, marvelously camouflaged, is a scorpionfish,* Scorpaenopsis venosa, *which remains stationary while it waits for its prey to pass.*

B - Characteristic of the coral seabeds, a tropical tasseled scorpionfish, Scorpaenopsis oxycephala, *is a perfect example of the mimetic skills and poisonous spines that make the family to which it belongs so dangerous.*

C - Normally peaceful, many sharks can become aggressive under certain circumstances. Among the species considered potentially dangerous is the silvertip shark, Carcharhinus albimarginatus, *which is characteristic of the deep reefs and is rare in the waters of Malaysia.*

D - The false stonefish, Scorpaenopsis diabolus, *perfectly camouflaged on the detrital substrata, can be dangerous to careless divers.*

with a tiger shark, *Galeocerdo cuvier*, objectively regarded as a dangerous shark, but this is an extremely remote possibility. In any event, sharks are certainly more curious and aggressive at night than during the day. Barracuda, despite their ferocious expression, are generally timid, but if you approach them in murky waters it is better to avoid wearing colorful or shiny objects, which they may confuse with the reflection of a potential prey. Also be careful not to approach the large stingrays, *Taeniura melanospilos*, from the rear, as their robust tails have one or more serrated stingers connected to a poison-producing gland. If you see one arching and rhythmically twitching its whiplike tail above its back, it is about to strike, with potentially fatal results. The rays of the dorsal and pectoral fins of the various scorpionfish and turkeyfish (*Scorpaenopsis* sp., *Pterois volitans* and *Pterois radiata*) are also very poisonous, although it is easy to avoid problems by not disturbing these animals. Also highly poisonous is the feared stonefish, *Synanceia verrucosa*, which is perfectly camouflaged on the shallow seabeds (divers should thus avoid walking in shallow water, even when wearing wetsuit shoes).

Sea snakes (those in the genus *Laticauda*, common near the mainland, are extremely poisonous) can also be somewhat curious or aggressive, and divers should always avoid disturbing and especially touching them. The morays (*Gymnothorax* sp.) can deliver serious and painful bites if disturbed in their lairs, so divers should never thoughtlessly put their hands into recesses or crevices. As with diving anywhere, divers in Malaysia will normally incur no injury if they keep their hands to themselves and avoid disturbing or touching underwater creatures. Some divers' tendency to touch or ride on marine animals, such as mantas and turtles, annoys and frightens them, forcing them to needlessly and dangerously flee. In addition, numerous organisms (sponges, hydroids, medusas and corals) have enhanced stinging properties which can trigger violent allergic reactions if touched with the bare skin. The most irritating species (apart from the well-known *Millepora*, or fire coral) are rather difficult to distinguish underwater.

These are all good reasons to avoid heedlessly grasping things. Such behavior can also cause serious damage to the coral reef; sometimes it takes only a clumsy kick of a fin or the touch of a gloved hand to destroy an entire community of organisms hundreds of years old. Most of the time man is the only truly dangerous animal underwater.

G

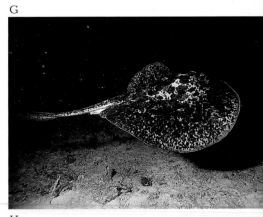

H

I

E

E - This close-up provides a good look at the pointed "beak" of a parrotfish. Harmless to humans, it can chew and destroy large blocks of coral.

F - Well known to aquarium fans and those familiar with tropical waters, the turkeyfish, Pterois volitans, is a beautiful subject for underwater photographers. Nevertheless, like all scorpionfish, it too is capable of inflicting extremely painful stings with the poisonous spines of its dorsal and pectoral fins.

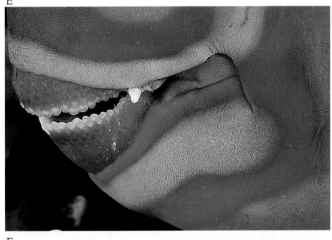

F

G - Like all its relatives, this large stingray, Taeniura melanospilos, has a dangerous toothed stinger located at the base of its tail, where it connects to a poison-producing gland. All the large rays of the genera Himantura, Taeniura and Dasyatis should always be approached from the front and never from behind.

H - The crown of thorns starfish, Acanthaster plancii, is covered with hard, pointed spines capable of causing very painful wounds. In addition, the mucus that covers them can cause infections which are difficult to heal.

I - The stingers of the sea urchin can cause painful wounds which are easily infected. Here is an elegant jewel box sea urchin, Tripneustes gratilla.

11

PULAU SIPADAN

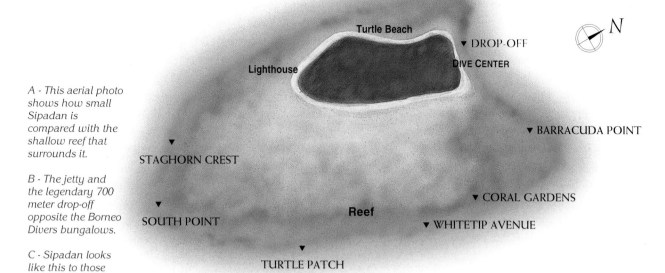

Turtle Beach
Lighthouse
▼ DROP-OFF
DIVE CENTER
N
▼ BARRACUDA POINT
▼
STAGHORN CREST
▼ CORAL GARDENS
▼
SOUTH POINT
Reef
▼ WHITETIP AVENUE
▼
TURTLE PATCH

A - This aerial photo shows how small Sipadan is compared with the shallow reef that surrounds it.

B - The jetty and the legendary 700 meter drop-off opposite the Borneo Divers bungalows.

C - Sipadan looks like this to those who arrive by sea from Semporna, about an hour's sail away.

A

B
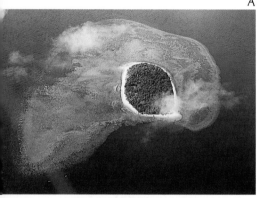

C

Pulau ("island") Sipadan is a patch of sand only 16 hectares in area, covered with a luxuriant, untouched rain forest. It is located five degrees north of the Equator, a little more than one hour's sail (32 kilometers) from the coastal city of Semporna in Malaysian Borneo, yet at the same time it is infinitely distant from our world.

What makes it so special? First of all, its geographical position: it is in the center of the richest marine habitat in the world, the heart of the Indo-Pacific basin. More than 3,000 species of fish have been classified here (compared with, for example, 780 species of fish in Indonesia's Ambon Bay alone, and 123 species of damselfish in the whole of Indonesia!), plus hundreds of species of corals. One reason for this is that the entire region has been uninterruptedly tropical for the last 100 million years, and the mass extinctions caused by the great glaciers a million years ago never occurred here.

A fortunate and rare combination of geophysical and environmental factors have also contributed to its astounding biological richness: its relative isolation (often it is not even indicated on maps and it is too far from the coast to be easily

reached by the fishermen's *prahu*, which in the past avoided the area for fear of pirates) and its structure (it is on the summit of a steep underwater mountain that rises almost vertically from an abyss of 700 meters and is separated from solid ground and the continental shelf by an arm of the sea more than 1,000 meters deep; toward the ocean depths of the Sea of Celebes the seabed is actually more than 2,000 meters deep) have made it both a sanctuary for numerous species threatened by human activity and an irresistible attraction for large schools of pelagic predators, as often occurs in isolated pinnacles in the open sea.

The origins of Pulau Sipadan date back to the Pliocene, when the intense volcanic activity of the Quaternary period created the peninsula of Semporna. The island's geological life, however, continued to be troubled. We know that erosion is responsible for the formation of atolls, molding them into their present shape. But the underwater caverns with stalagmites and stalactites that open into Pulau Sipadan's submerged walls and the narrow underwater shelf that encircles it like a balcony at a depth of about 30 meters, the remains of an ancient beach, suggest that about 20,000 years ago the island was much higher above sea level than it is today. At present it is no more than two meters above sea level, with a maximum reef width of more than two kilometers.

Over recent years the name of Pulau Sipadan has become legendary in diving circles. Due to the visitors' facilities that Borneo Divers, followed by two other operators, built on the island - sufficiently rustic to have limited human impact on the environment - today the underwater beauty of the island and its amazing richness is shared by visitors and researchers from all over the world.

The extent to which continuous visits to its seabeds may damage it in years to come is the subject of cautious debate. So far it is certain that while there has been a negligible deterioration of a few meters of coral reef, the number of species sighted has increased significantly, with a remarkable decrease in shyness in the creatures encountered while diving. With its 10 different diving sites, all located along the perimeter of the island and reachable by light fiberglass outboard motorboats in just a few minutes, every day divers can see hundreds of *Chelonia mydas* and *Eretmochelys imbricata* turtles (which have courted and mated on the seabeds of Sipadan for thousands of years, depositing their eggs in the sands of its beaches), immense schools of great barracuda, *Sphyraena barracuda*, and bigeye trevallies, *Caranx sexfasciatus*, hordes of

F

G

giant bumphead parrotfish, *Bolbometopon muricatum*, phalanxes of scalloped hammerhead sharks, *Sphyrna lewini*, the flights of mantas, *Manta birostris*, and eagle rays, *Aetobatus narinari*, small groups of grey reef sharks, *Carcharhinus amblyrhynchos*, innumerable whitetip reef sharks, *Triaenodon obesus*, and leopard sharks, *Stegostoma fasciatum*, and a seemingly infinite number of species of reef fauna. This includes a plethora of fish, such as gobies, scorpionfish, groupers and triggerfish, not to mention crustaceans, mollusks, sponges and corals of every shape and size. The giant or coconut crabs, *Birgus latro*, a few hundred of which live in the rain forest, are also of interest, as are the rare mound birds, *Megapodius cummingii*, and the Nicobar pigeon, *Caloenas nicobarica*, which nests here (along with forty-six other species of birds thus far reported, despite the absence of permanent sources of fresh water on the island) and the island flying fox, *Pteropus hypomelanus*, with a "wing-span" of over 24 inches.

D

E

D - Great numbers of whip gorgonians from the genus Elisella, with their characteristic scarlet color, adorn the deep waters of Sipadan and host many types of symbiotic species.

E - Numerous large colonies of sea fans from the genus Melithaea can also be found in the deep waters off Sipadan.

F - Characteristic of these seabeds are schools of bigeye trevallies, Caranx sexfasciatus, *and striped barracuda,* Sphyraena putnamiae, *which often gather in vortices of hundreds of individuals.*

G - Sea turtles are the symbol of Pulau Sipadan, where it is not uncommon to see 15-20 during a single dive. This is a green turtle, Chelonia mydas.

THE DROP-OFF

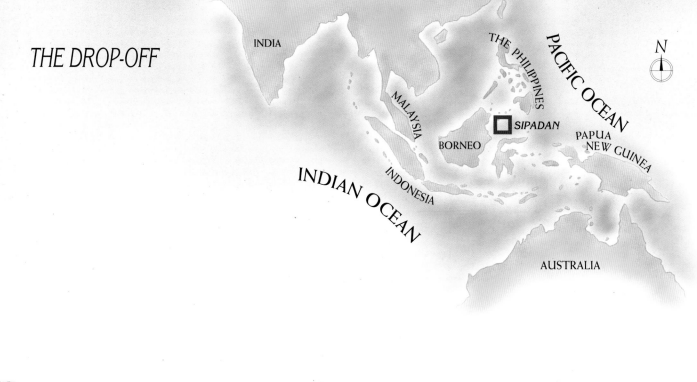

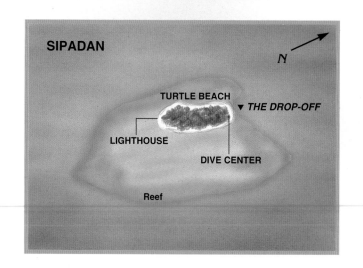

SIPADAN

TURTLE BEACH

THE DROP-OFF

LIGHTHOUSE

DIVE CENTER

Reef

N

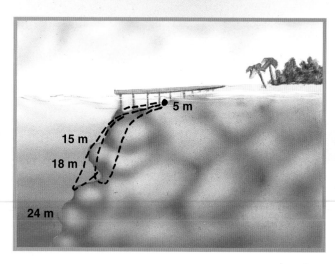

5 m

15 m

18 m

24 m

0 m

5 m

15 m

18 m

24 m

B

Few diving sites in the world are as famous as the legendary Sipadan Drop-Off. Its fame is well-deserved - where else in the world is it possible to get on your knees in water a half a meter deep, put on your mask and look down into a dizzying vertical drop of over 700 meters, with sharks and turtles passing each other peacefully a few meters below? This dive begins on the beach opposite the Borneo Divers diving center.

Divers suit up in the diving center itself, just a few meters from the sea, or in the water. After going about 20 meters in waist-deep water, they are faced with numerous alternatives, all equally

A - Sipadan is famous the world over for its vertiginous Drop-Off. It plunges straight down for more than 700 meters, providing thrilling dives at any depth.

B - Encounters with large schools of bigeye trevallies, Caranx sexfasciatus, *especially groups of immature or young individuals, are not uncommon along The Drop-Off.*

C - The crevices that open up into the walls of The Drop-Off are frequented by numerous sea turtles, such as this female turtle, from the genus Chelonia mydas, *recognizable by the rounded snout and small tail.*

D - A rare sight among the coral formations of the drop-off is the giant cuttlefish, Sepia pharaonis, *shown in the photograph.*

A

C

D

exciting. Depending on the light available, the prevailing currents and the number of dives already completed that day, they can opt for a deep dive with a gradual diagonal ascent, a horizontal exploration at medium depth or a relaxing observation of reef life right at the edge of The Drop-Off, at two to five meters deep. The area offers absolutely extraordinary opportunities by day and night. Indeed, The Drop-Off is essentially the only site at Pulau Sipadan where it is possible to make night dives, and is the only one that can be explored directly from the beach.

If normal precautions are taken, it is an easy dive that anyone can enjoy. However, it is important not to stray too far from the wall and to be careful of approaching motorboats (the island's mooring dock was built right along The Drop-Off). Another potential hazard is drifting too far horizontally along the wall. If divers keep it on their right they will end up at Barracuda Point. Following the wall to their left will take them to the North Point, beyond which West Ridge begins. Both areas may have very strong currents, making it difficult if not impossible to get back.

Although anything is possible at Sipadan and encounters with pelagic species are frequent in the blue depths beyond The Drop-Off, it is ideal for macrophotography, especially at night. Far from being uniform, the wall is a constant succession of little grottos, cavities, cracks, balconies and terraces teeming with life. At a depth of about 20 meters there is a wide cavern, nicknamed "Turtle Tomb", which divers can explore only at the discretion of, and if they are accompanied by, a local divemaster. It is littered with the skeletons of turtles which drowned after failing to find their way out. Several unsupervised divers have reportedly met the same fate.

In addition to the usual extraordinary range of reef fauna, we should also mention the firefish, *Nemateleotris magnifica*, and the less common but similar

E

F

G

E - The top of The Drop-Off hosts an astounding quantity of species characteristic of the reef, including the tiny, brightly colored striped fangblenny, Plagiotremus rhinorhynchos.

F - Along The Drop-Off you can see numerous lovely turkeyfish, Pterois sp., *with their vivid colors.*

G - Night dives are an opportunity to observe large, splendidly colored crustaceans such as the Carpilius convexus *crab.*

A - The crevices and cavities of The Drop-Off host numerous large anemones from the genus Heteractis, *from which peer their symbiotic clownfish, in this case* Amphiprion ocellaris.

B - The large fans of the gorgonians stretched out into the current often offer an ideal position for filtering creatures such as crinoids.

Nemateleotris decora, rare morays (generally *Gymnothorax*) and numerous *Radianthus* and *Stoichachtis* anemones inhabited by a large number (at least nine different species have been observed to date) of symbiotic clownfish from the genus *Amphiprion*. Among the branches of the gorgonians, which are sometimes unusually large, may be tiny, beautiful gobies, while in the immediate vicinity of the fixed mooring line used by the boats, schools of reef squid from the genus

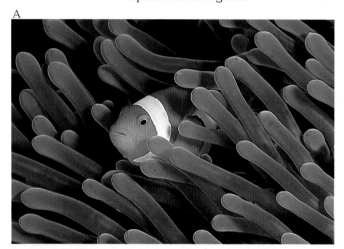

Sepioteuthis often hover, suspended near the surface like a myriad of tiny spaceships in formation. All around swim large turtles, *Chelonia mydas*, waiting to climb up the beach at night to deposit their eggs, and whitetip reef sharks, *Triaenodon obesus*, large solitary barracuda, *Sphyraena barracuda*, and in the larger crevices or on the flat areas of the reef, dense whirls of young bigeye trevallies, *Caranx sexfasciatus*, and immense schools of multi-hued

C - A careful observation of the corals at Sipadan is likely to reveal the perfectly camouflaged form of a multi-hued tropical tasseled scorpionfish, Scorpaenopsis oxycephala.

E

diversity of species make the Sipadan Drop-Off one of the world's most spectacular diving sites. But given the large number of sometimes careless divers who visit it day and night, a real effort must be made to protect the coral formations and their inhabitants so that it continues to deserve its international reputation.

E - Schools of barracuda, Sphyraena putnamiae, may be seen anywhere along the reef of Sipadan, although they appear to prefer South Point and Barracuda Point.

F - Between 30 and 40 meters deep, it is not uncommon to encounter a grey reef shark, Carcharhinus amblyrynchos. This species is territorial and may attack intruders.

G - Smaller in size and easier to approach, the whitetip reef shark, Triaenodon obesus, can be surprisingly fast, especially at night.

D - The small grottos and balconies that open up into The Drop-Off between 4 and 20 meters deep are the preferred night-time rest areas for the gigantic bumphead parrotfish, Bolbometopon muricatum.

Pseudanthias. Under the dock are groups of young batfish, *Platax teira*, and among the fragments of dead coral on the sandy bottom, false stonefish. At night, in addition to the seemingly countless crustaceans (the most common are the *Stenopus hispidus* shrimps, but there are also much rarer species in the genus *Periclemenes* and *Saron*) and reef predators in search of prey (especially scorpionfish, and in the open water, whitetip reef sharks), are numerous specimens of green turtles and gigantic bumphead parrotfish, *Bolbometopon muricatum*, sleeping in cavities in the wall. It is also common to see small flashlight fish, *Photoblepharon palpebratus*, which in the dark look like a magical swarm of fireflies, small scorpionfish, *Dendrochirus biocellatus*, and razorfish from the genus *Centriscus*, hidden among the branches of the gorgonians.
This extraordinary richness and

F

G

BARRACUDA POINT

INDIA

THE PHILIPPINES

PACIFIC OCEAN

MALAYSIA

SIPADAN

BORNEO

PAPUA NEW GUINEA

INDONESIA

INDIAN OCEAN

AUSTRALIA

N

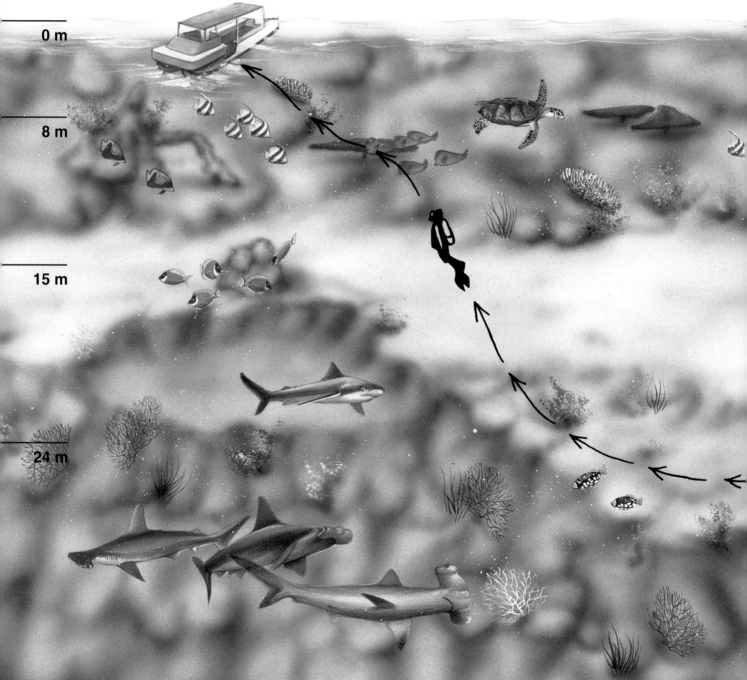

0 m

8 m

15 m

24 m

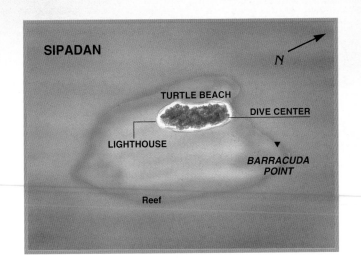

SIPADAN

TURTLE BEACH

DIVE CENTER

LIGHTHOUSE

BARRACUDA POINT

Reef

N

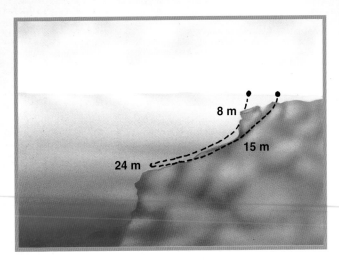

8 m

15 m

24 m

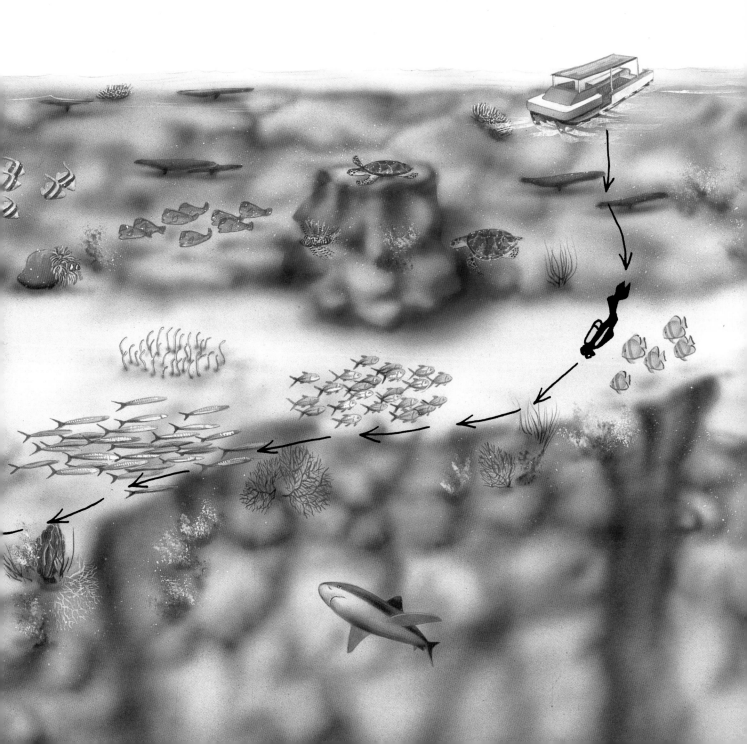

Along with South Point and the Sipadan drop-off, this is one of the most spectacular dives possible on Sipadan. Generally divers enter the water at the eastern tip of the Sipadan drop-off, with the current in their favor and keeping the wall to their right. The dive begins along a spectacular, nearly vertical wall adorned with large festoons of gorgonians. As divers descend to about 40 meters, they are likely to see individual or small groups of grey reef sharks, *Carcharhinus amblyrhynchos*, and scalloped hammerhead sharks, *Sphyrna lewini*. At shallower depths, or even near the surface, as soon as they enter the water, they may well see spectacular "orgies" of *Chelonia mydas* turtles - various males, sometimes as many as six or seven, contending for a single female - or an impressive school of giant bumphead parrotfish, *Bolbometopon muricatum*, grazing tranquilly on the reef. Carried on the increasingly strong current (which may sometimes unexpectedly carry

C

D

A - At Barracuda Point, one of the most spectacular diving sites at Sipadan, there are numerous turtles from the genera Chelonia mydas (shown in the photograph) and Eretmochelys imbricata.

B - The spectacular schools of barracuda, Sphyraena putnamiae, habitually frequent this stretch of reef, which is continuously swept by strong currents.

C - A diver swims below a wall of silvery bigeye trevallies, which are quite frequent in these waters.

D - By avoiding abrupt movements and keeping the emission of air bubbles to a minimum, more experienced divers can even swim into the living walls of the barracuda and mingle with these splendid predators.

A

B

divers down and out to the open sea, so inexperienced ones should be careful), they will reach a series of balconies that open out to the blue depths on one side, and on the other frame a sort of large sandy arena about 30 meters deep. Here, resting on the seabed, are numerous whitetip reef sharks, *Triaenodon obesus*, and turtles. Despite the name of the area, the huge vortices of thousands of great barracuda, *Sphyraena barracuda*, are a rarer sight. At this point divers conclude their exhilarating ride on the current, which by now has become quite strong, and ascend diagonally towards the slope to their right, passing a large sandy gully. The dive ends at another site appropriately called Coral Gardens. This is the most difficult part of the dive, because in some areas it will be necessary to swim against the current. Divers should be calm yet determined and forceful, to avoid being carried out into the open sea. The last part of the dive, including the safety stop, can be devoted to observing the fauna of the reef,

E

E - The strong currents that sweep Barracuda Point attract large concentrations of fish, such as this school of blue-tailed unicornfish, Naso hexacanthus.

F - Either alone or in small groups, goggle-eyes, Priacanthus hamrur, *are everywhere along the reef of Sipadan, often in the shadow of the colonies of plate* Acropora.

G - What would be exceptional elsewhere is not uncommon at Barracuda Point: a great swarm of gigantic parrotfish, Bolbometopon muricatum, *which daily makes its way around the perimeter of the island.*

which here is particularly full of delicate madrepore formations (*Acropora splendida, nobilis* and *hyacinthus, Pavona cactus* and *Turbinaria*), large soft corals (*Sarcophyton, Lobophytum* and *Xenia*), gaudy creatures such as the numerous species of *Amphiprion* clownfish, triggerfish, grunts, groupers, turkeyfish, butterflyfish, lobsters and, of course, the inevitable turtles. Visibility at Barracuda Point is generally good but it varies greatly depending on the currents and the time of year.
Although this dive site is accessible to everyone, it probably requires the most experience of all those at Sipadan.

F

G

H

I

H - The sandy seabeds of Barracuda Point are a sure place to encounter numerous whitetip reef sharks, Triaenodon obesus.

I - The waters of Barracuda Point are often traveled by schools of elegant Boers batfish, Platax boersii, *easily recognizable by their yellowish caudal fin.*

CORAL GARDENS

INDIA

THE PHILIPPINES

PACIFIC OCEAN

MALAYSIA

SIPADAN

BORNEO

PAPUA
NEW GUINEA

INDONESIA

INDIAN OCEAN

AUSTRALIA

N

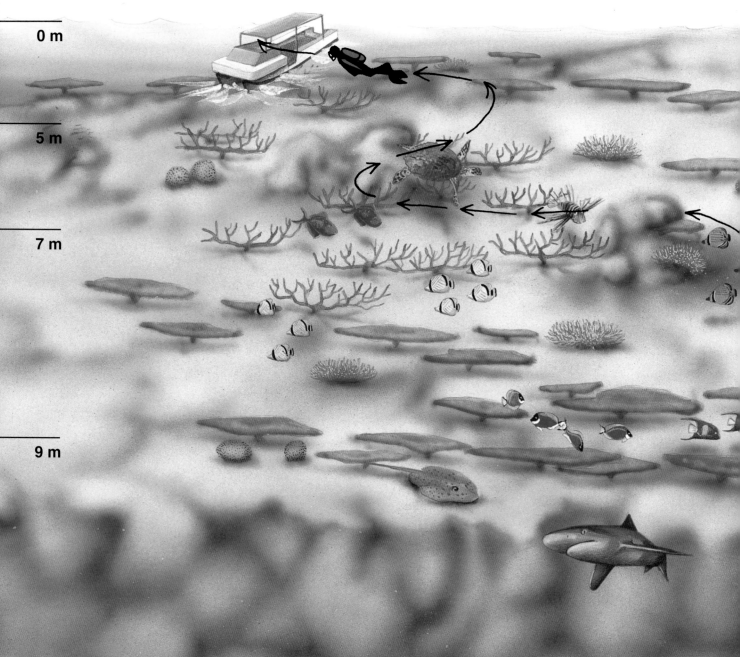

0 m

5 m

7 m

9 m

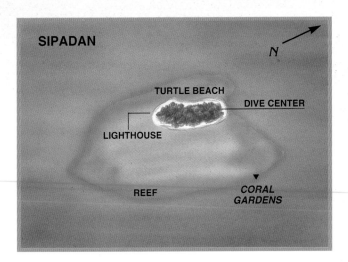

SIPADAN

N

TURTLE BEACH

LIGHTHOUSE

DIVE CENTER

REEF

CORAL GARDENS

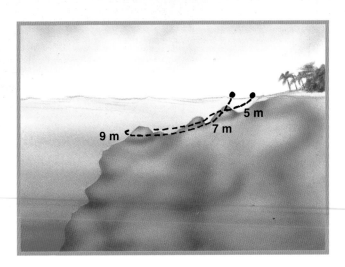

9 m   7 m   5 m

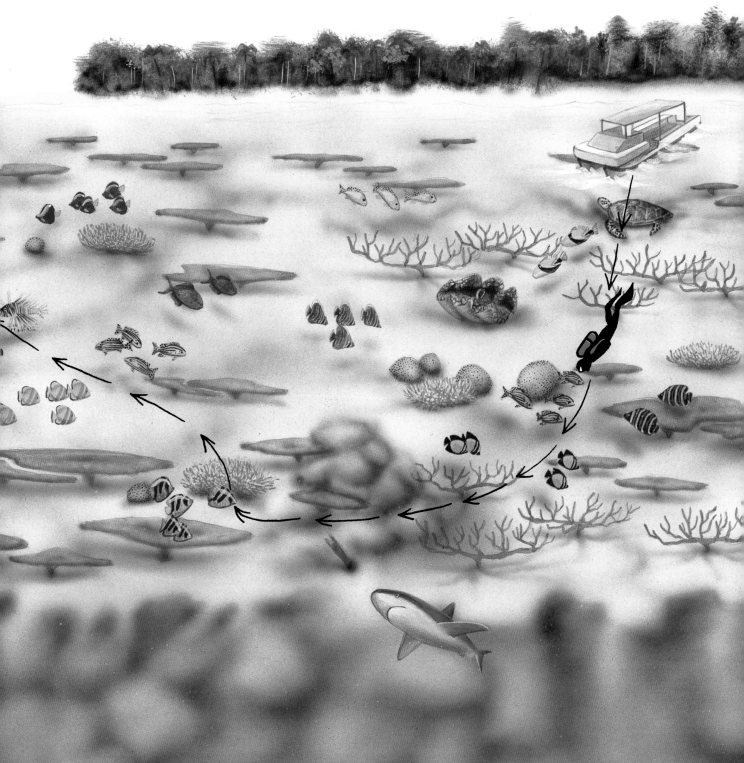

Rarely considered a destination in and of itself, Coral Gardens is usually visited at the conclusion of a dive at Barracuda Point, as its shallow seabeds and luxuriant coral formations are ideal for a relaxed safety stop at a shallow depth. Nevertheless, demanding photographers should devote more than one dive to Coral Gardens, perhaps after exhausting the thrills that other sites at Sipadan offer. In these few hundred meters of reef, bordered by an abrupt slope or sandy gully that steeply drops into the open sea, the diversity of species is astounding. The shallow sandy seabed, between five and 10 meters deep, is dotted with an infinite variety of hard coral bommies, ancient colonies of *Porites* and *Turbinaria*, vigorous colonies of brain coral and intricate and fragile "thickets" of *Acropora splendida* and *nobilis* staghorn corals, with complex, labyrinthine mazes of *Pavona cactus* lettuce coral.

All around, busy with the thousand

A - The shallow reef at Coral Gardens is extraordinarily full of life and color.

B - A careful examination of the area shaded by the coral formations reveals pairs of racoon butterflyfish, Chaetodon lunula.

C - Due to its strange coloration, the clown triggerfish, Balistoides conspicillum, is one of the reef's most showy and colorful inhabitants.

C

A

D

B

activities involved in daily survival, reef fish in every shape and color move, dart, shine and glitter in the bright water. As with diving at any of the shallow coral reefs surrounding Sipadan, it feels like swimming in the warm, tranquil waters of a tropical aquarium, with a variety of animal species that is truly incredible. Positioned all around in their particular ecological niches, the inhabitants of the reef reveal themselves to divers one after another: butterflyfish from the

D - The blue-faced angelfish, Pomacanthus xanthometapon, also boasts brilliant colors. Encounters with its relative, the emperor angelfish, are also common at Coral Gardens.

genus *Chaetodon* in small groups or in pairs near coral formations; their larger relatives, angelfish in the genus *Pomacanthus*, busy defending their territory against real or presumed invaders with grunts and vigorous offensive thrusts, triggerfish from the genera *Balistes* and *Balistoides*, hovering head down above their nests dug in the sand, busy protecting freshly deposited eggs or rummaging on the sea floor, and wrasses, very different from each other depending on species, sex and even age, darting here and there like harried commuters who are running late.

There are also large groups of sweetlips, from the genus *Plectorhynchus*, immobile in the shadow of large colonies of *Porites* and brain corals, blue-spotted ribbontail stingrays, *Taeniura lymma*, half-buried in the sand, with splendid electric blue ocelli on their mustard-colored backs, *Pterois volitans* and *Pterois radiata* turkeyfish lying in wait among the coral branches, suspended in the void, and large tropical scorpionfish from the genus *Scorpaenopsis*, perfectly camouflaged on the coral. The richness of the area is extraordinary: with a little attention and a bit of luck, the diver may even see the small and fascinating leaf scorpionfish, *Taenianotus triacanthus*, oscillating in the shade of the corals, the lair of a rare, elegant ribbon eel, *Rhynomuraena quaesita*, or the hole from which peeps the vividly colored and shy mantis prawn, *Odontodactylus scyllaris*, the garishly colored tropical relative of the Mediterranean mantis prawn.

E - More similar to a living jewel than a fish, the spotted turkeyfish, Pterois antennata, *slides among the corals in search of prey.*

F - Extremely common along the entire reef of Sipadan, at all depths, crinoids add bright touches of color.

G - Multicolored when illuminated by the camera flash, yet perfectly camouflaged in the light of the sun, a large tasseled scorpionfish, Scorpaenopsis oxycephala, *lies immobile as it awaits its prey.*

H - A large anemone, Heteractis magnifica, *with an* unusual violet color, hosts a family of anemone fish, *Amphiprion perideraion.*

I - The extremely elegant blue ribbon eel, Rhinomuraena quaesita, *much more common on the seabeds of nearby Pulau Mabul, is a rare encounter in the waters of Sipadan.*

WHITETIP AVENUE

INDIA

THE PHILIPPINES

PACIFIC OCEAN

MALAYSIA

☐ SIPADAN

BORNEO

PAPUA
NEW GUINEA

INDONESIA

INDIAN OCEAN

AUSTRALIA

N

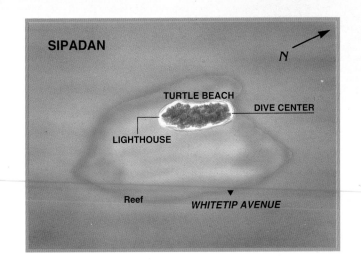

SIPADAN

N

TURTLE BEACH

DIVE CENTER

LIGHTHOUSE

Reef

WHITETIP AVENUE

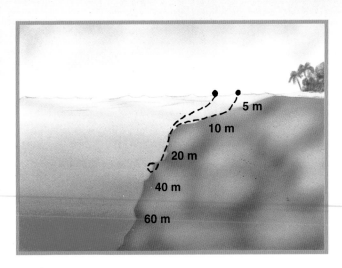

5 m

10 m

20 m

40 m

60 m

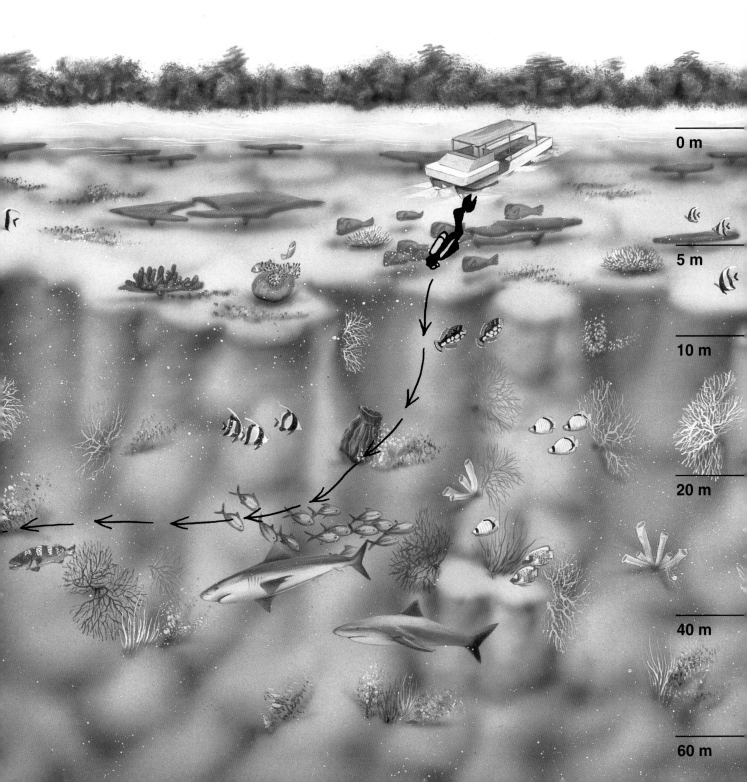

0 m

5 m

10 m

20 m

40 m

60 m

A

B

C

D

A - *Often ignored by divers, sponges are actually quite interesting for both naturalists and photographers.*

B - *The regal angelfish,* Pygoplites diacanthus, *boasts colors of rare beauty and elegance. Like all angelfish, it feeds on sponges and invertebrates.*

C - Pomacanthus sexstriatus *is an extremely beautiful angelfish that reaches a length of forty-five centimeters. However, it is not particularly showy and difficult to spot.*

D - *The many-spotted sweetlips,* Plectorhinchus chaetodonoides, *reaches sixty centimeters in length. At Sipadan it can be seen almost everywhere, often in small groups and generally at shallow depths.*

E - *This school of young of* Pseudanthias tuka, *or purple anthias, seeks protection among the branches of a gorgonian.*

Whitetip Avenue is a tremendous dive site along Sipadan's eastern wall. The particular route taken, however, depends on the direction of the current and is decided by the divemaster before entering the water from a motorboat.
In any case, the underwater orography is typical of the eastern side of Sipadan - a broad terrace full of corals and alcyonarians located at an extremely shallow depth that suddenly plunges into the abyss in a vertiginous, nearly vertical drop-off, among festoons of gigantic gorgonians and large colonies of black corals.
The classical diving scheme (initial dive to the bottom with a gradual

E

diagonal ascent, concluding with a safety stop at a shallow depth) is often interrupted by unexpected encounters as soon as the diver enters the water. Indeed, it is not uncommon for a diver to find himself in the middle of a large school of gigantic bumphead parrotfish, *Bolbometopon muricatum,* grazing methodically on the upper portion of the reef (the school methodically moves along the circumference of the island and spends the night in the grottos in the drop-off across from the Borneo Divers bungalows) or an extraordinary silver vortex of thousands of bigeye trevallies, *Caranx sexfasciatus.*
Alternatively, divers will descend

to about thirty meters, dividing their attention between the wall on one side and the open sea on the opposite side. Terraces, balconies, crevices and vertical chimneys punctuate the wall, which is full of sessile organisms - sponges in every shape and color, enormous gorgonians and large colonies of black coral - among which circles a myriad of reef and den fish, including groupers, emperor angelfish, Moorish idols, triggerfish, clownfish, boxfish, parrotfish, butterflyfish and multi-hued scorpionfish.

On the ocean side, the unexpected lies in wait: the sinuous, sinister form of a grey reef shark, *Carcharhinus amblyrhynchos* may rise out of the depths, or the rays of the sun may silhouette the majestic and rare spectacle of a great school of scalloped hammerhead sharks, *Sphyrna lewini*, which customarily patrols the deeper waters of Pulau Sipadan. If you are lucky enough to experience this, don't spoil it: hammerheads are quite timid, and swimming quickly toward them in an attempt to photograph them will only cause them to vanish into the deep in a fraction of a second. It is much better for divers to camouflage themselves against the wall and minimize the emission of bubbles in the hope that the great sharks will be curious enough to approach for a quick exploratory visit.

A gradual diagonal ascent will finally carry divers to the coral gardens of Turtle Patch, an extremely elegant, sandy, flat area teeming with life. They can relax and watch this while being carried to a depth of just a few meters by the vigorous current which is almost always present, until they surface near the support boat waiting at about 20 meters from the edge of the reef.

F

G

H

I

F - The hawkfish, Oxycirrhites typus, is a tiny predator characteristic of deep waters, and normally lives associated with the large colonies of black corals from the genus Antipatharia.

G - The small pufferfish, Canthigaster valentini, can easily be observed as it moves rapidly and jerkily among the corals at shallow and medium depths.

H - At Sipadan the grey reef sharks, Carcharhinus amblyrynchos, prefer vertical drop-offs at least 30 meters deep.

I - The great sedentary school of scalloped hammerhead sharks, Sphyrna lewini, lives permanently at depths greater than 40 meters. Nevertheless, sometimes the school rises to shallower depths when the water temperature drops.

31

TURTLE PATCH

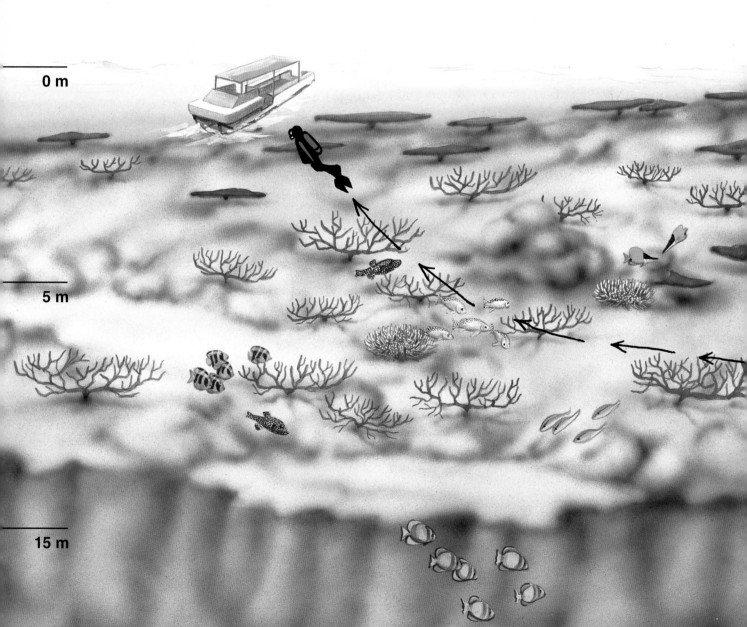

0 m

5 m

15 m

SIPADAN

N

TURTLE BEACH

DIVE CENTER

LIGHTHOUSE

Reef

TURTLE PATCH

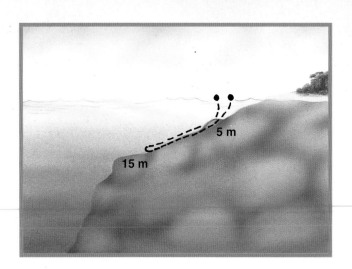

5 m

15 m

Turtle Patch, along with Coral Gardens, is the best site in Sipadan for a shallow dive using the hovering technique. Divers gently glide on the current that allows them to survey from a stationary position the luxuriant, delicate coral formations characteristic of the island's shallow seabeds, which are extremely common here.
The site is often not considered a diving destination in itself, and most often is reached and crossed on the current following a dive at South Point or, from the opposite side, Midreef or Whitetip Avenue. This is really a mistake, because given its particular conformation Turtle Patch should certainly not be underestimated. Indeed, it provides divers and marine biology buffs with unique opportunities. The upper plateau is not shaded by any vertical drop-off, and thus it is fully illuminated both in the morning and afternoon. This feature, along with the area's flat, basically sandy and detrital character, sloping into broad

B

C

C - A family of symbiotic anemonefish, Amphiprion perideraion, *lives and finds a safe refuge among the tentacles of this large anemone from the genus* Heteractis.

D - This splendid example of a giant moray, Gymnothorax javanicus, *peeps out of its lair, adorned with a cascade of pink alcyonarians.*

E - This photograph shows the delicate structure of the fins of the scorpionfish, one of the loveliest but most fearsome of the reef's inhabitants.

A

D

terraces toward the eastern wall, has permitted splendid colonies of hard corals to establish themselves (including *Acropora splendida* and *nobilis, Acropora hyacinthus, Pavona cactus* and *Turbinaria*), along with soft corals from the genera *Sarcophyton* and *Xenia,* among which giant turtles glide, oblivious of visiting divers. Indeed, these creatures, often quietly resting among the soft corals instead of feeding greedily on large sponges, are more common here than elsewhere in Sipadan.
The large tabular terraces of *Acropora* also offer a safe refuge for groups of spotted grunts (also known as sweetlips), and goatfish from the genus *Parupeneus,* while among the branches of the staghorn corals and under the flat formations of *Acropora,* may be large isolated specimens of burrfish, *Diodon hystrix,* spotted pufferfish, *Arothron,* and pairs of yellow and black *Siganus vulpinus.*
All around circle groups of *Chaetodon* butterflyfish,

A - The stretches of reef most affected by the current are also the preferred habitat of

alcyonarians from the genus Dendronephthya, *perhaps the most spectacular of the so-called soft corals.*

B - This sponge stretched out into the blue depths is being used by a crinoid as a handy perch to facilitate feeding.

34

F - Perfectly camouflaged on the detrital substratum, a leaf scorpionfish, Taenianothus triacanthus, *in its white color phase, displays some of the most fascinating colors and forms in the underwater world.*

G - A group of yellowstriped goatfish, Mulloides vanicolensis, *methodically combs the reef in search of nourishment.*

H - A large map puffer, Arothron mappa, *rests in the shade of a plate coral from the genus* Acropora, *as is customary in this species. Pufferfish have extremely strong teeth which can cause serious wounds.*

I - Peacefully resting among the corals, a beautiful turtle, from the genus Chelonia mydas, *observes the photographer. The turtles are called "green" because of the color of their fat, not their shells.*

characteristically timid, multi-hued tropical groupers, capricious triggerfish and many other species typical of the reef. Numerous large sea anemones populated by groups of clown anemonefish and their shrimp complete the exciting scene.

Sometimes, moving toward the balconies that mark the beginning of the drop-off, divers may meet a leopard shark, *Stegostoma fasciatum*, sleeping in the sand, or a large ray from the genus *Taeniura*. But the best way to appreciate Turtle Patch is to simply remain near the surface and be carried by the current - which is sometimes quite strong, with unpredictable variations in horizontal visibility - while carefully observing the coral seabed moving by just a short distance below.

Lucky divers may encounter rare species like the lovely leaf scorpionfish, *Taenianotus triacanthus*, which may vary from bright yellow to violet to more common cream and brown colors,

F

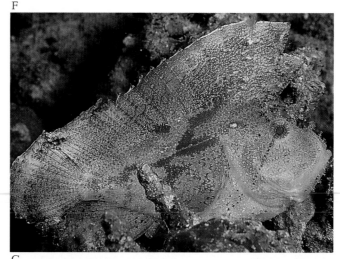

G

E

H

I

depending on the substratum it chooses for its territory.

A word of advice: due to the very shallow depth of the site, divers should move away from the reef as they surface to avoid inadvertently damaging the luxuriant but extremely delicate coral formations with a clumsy blow of a fin.

SOUTH POINT

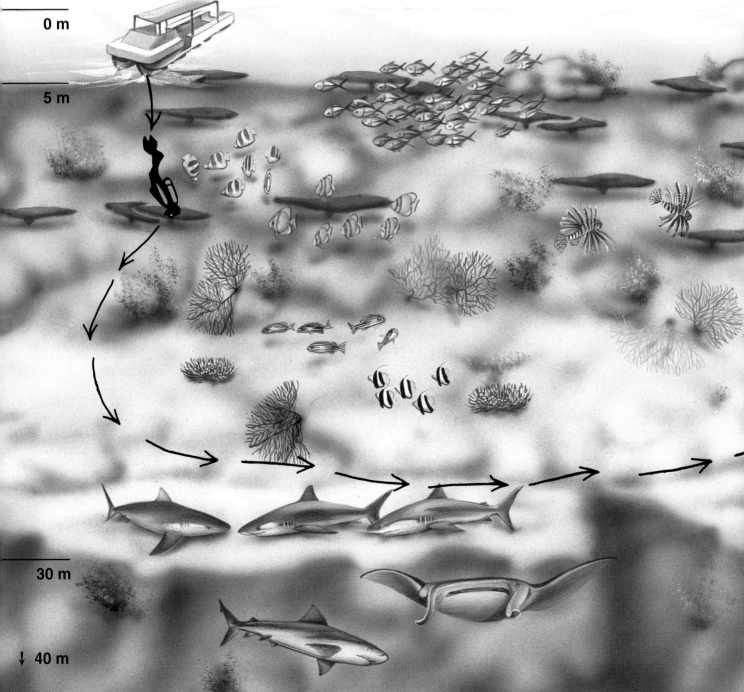

0 m

5 m

30 m

↓ 40 m

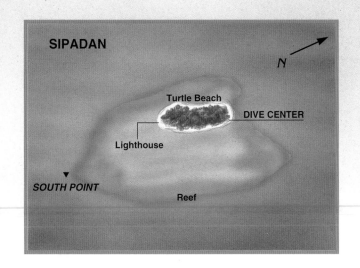

SIPADAN

Turtle Beach

DIVE CENTER

Lighthouse

SOUTH POINT

Reef

N

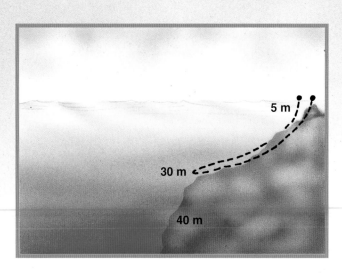

5 m

30 m

40 m

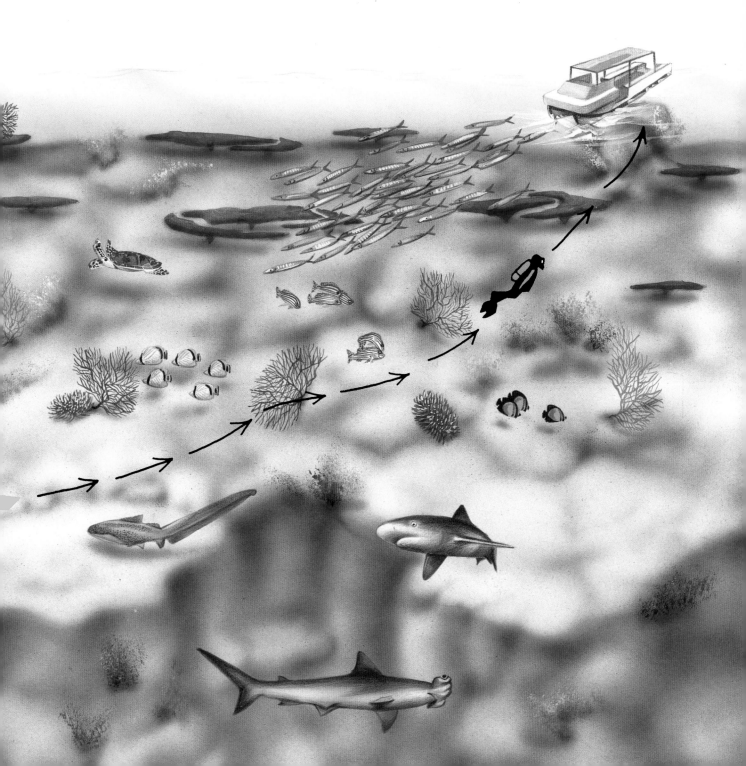

A - Dives in the waters of South Point offer the chance to admire dense schools of passing fish. This photo shows several silvery batfish elegantly crossing the depths.

L ocated at the southern tip of Pulau Sipadan, South Point is a particularly popular diving site because it is one of the best places for spectacular encounters. Divers should enter the water just beyond the site known as Staghorn Crest, with the current at their back and the wall to their left. Here the drop-off is at about 45 degrees, and the slope, with no particularly spectacular coral formations, slides down toward a flat, sandy area of coral fragments located at

C

D

A

B

a depth of about 60 meters, and then continues towards the open sea to much greater depths. Leopard sharks, *Stegostoma fasciatum*, often quite large, can frequently be seen resting on the flat area of shattered corals. Continuing in a diagonal ascent, divers come to a group of terraces of shattered coral at a depth of 30 meters. These balconies are the preferred haunts of numerous whitetip reef sharks, *Triaenodon obesus*, which rest here in groups of four or five. Photographers will enjoy stopping here: if they are cautious they can approach the sharks for unusual close-ups. Divers continue to ascend diagonally until arriving at the splendid coral gardens at the southern tip, only a few meters deep. Here are numerous reef species such as *Chelonia mydas* or *Eretmochelys imbricata* turtles, which can often be observed as they feed on soft corals; large groups of *Platax* batfish and *Plectorynchus* sweetlips; juvenile whitetip sharks hidden under the coral umbrellas; turkeyfish, *Pterois*

B - At South Point as well as everywhere along the reefs of Sipadan, it is possible to approach and observe at close range numerous splendid specimens of turtles, from the genus Chelonia mydas, *which unfortunately have become rare elsewhere.*

C - The leaf scorpionfish, Taenianothus triacanthus, *prefers sheltered areas and detrital substrata. Once it has chosen its territory it never leaves, and thus it can be observed in the same place for many years.*

D - South Point offers excellent opportunities to approach a large number of whitetip reef sharks, Triaenodon obesus, *as they rest on a detrital seabed about 15 meters deep.*

E - South Point often hosts a living cyclone of hundreds of bigeye trevallies, Caranx sexfasciatus.

F - This photo shows a vortex of hundreds of bigeye trevallies. If you swim carefully without making any abrupt movements, you can mingle with them and take memorable photographs.

volitans, on the hunt; rare leaf scorpionfish, *Taenionotus triacanthus,* admirably camouflaged among the corals; and with a bit of luck, even a leopard shark resting on the sand. The diving itinerary at South Point, however, is often radically changed by the presence of spectacular vortices of bigeye trevallies, *Caranx sexfasciatus,* and great barracuda, *Sphyraena barracuda,* that have made the island world famous - real cyclones of thousands of fish, among which divers can hover, surrounded by a great, whirling, seething, silvery mass.
As if that were not enough, South Point is also one of the best places to see the large pelagic species that frequent the island's waters: solitary whale sharks, *Rinchodon typus,* manta rays, *Manta borostris,* or eagle rays, *Aetobatus narinari,* and the gigantic school of scalloped hammerhead sharks, *Sphyrna lewini,* that incessantly patrols the deeper waters.

G

H

I

E

F

G - A rare and fortunate event, an encounter with a giant manta, Manta birostris, *is an unforgettable thrill. As with all large pelagic filtering species, March and April are the best months for a sighting.*

H - An encounter with the large sedentary school of scalloped hammerhead sharks, Sphyrna lewini, *is a rare and unexpected event.*

I - The rarest sight you may see in the waters beyond South Point is a whale shark, Rhinchodon typus, *the largest fish in the world. Harmless and elegant, whale sharks feed on plankton.*

STAGHORN CREST

INDIA

THE PHILIPPINES

PACIFIC OCEAN

N

MALAYSIA

SIPADAN

BORNEO

PAPUA NEW GUINEA

INDONESIA

INDIAN OCEAN

AUSTRALIA

0 m

5 m

10 m

15 m

20 m

30 m

40 m

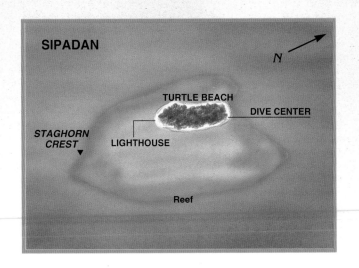

SIPADAN

N

TURTLE BEACH

DIVE CENTER

LIGHTHOUSE

STAGHORN
CREST

Reef

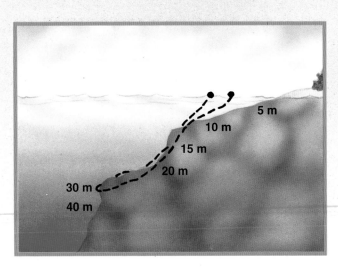

5 m

10 m

15 m

20 m

30 m

40 m

Another classic wall dive on Sipadan, Staghorn Crest offers excellent illumination during the afternoon hours (photographers take note). As is also the case for the adjacent sites of Hanging Gardens and Lobster Lairs, the dive at Staghorn Crest begins with a gentle descent along the drop-off (which begins just a few centimeters below the surface and proceeds with somewhat irregular grades and terraces until merging with a sandy flat area about sixty-seven meters deep) and continues with a gradual diagonal ascent along the wall, which is full of crevices, cavities, balconies and protruding vaults. It concludes in the staghorn coral garden at shallow depth that gives the area its name. Like the other wall dives of Sipadan, there are many lovely areas here. Lower down, divers who keep close to the wall can admire splendid colonies of red seawhip corals, gigantic barrel sponges, dense, luxuriant bushes of black corals and, close to the crevices in the wall, a large number of the most beautiful

B
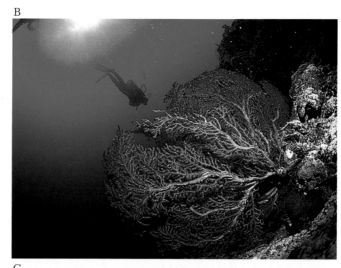

C

C - The dense colonies of whip gorgonians from the genus Elisella, *which appear brownish and insignificant in deep water, are a bright red color when illuminated by the camera flash.*

D - At depths of 15-40 meters, you can see lush colonies of black corals from the genus Antipathates, *with crowns that are sometimes two meters wide. This coral is the preferred habitat for numerous gobies and shrimps.*

A

D

A - Staghorn Crest, like all vertical drop-offs at Sipadan, hosts a large number of gigantic and spectacular specimens of barrel sponges, Xestospongia testudinaria.

B - The wall of Staghorn Crest, full of brightly colored gorgonians and lush colonies of black corals, offers an infinite variety of photo opportunities.

species in these waters. Splendid emperors whirl and circle from every cavity and balcony, along with little groups of angelfish, various species of groupers, grunts, *Lethrinidae* and triggerfish. Lovers of the reef microcosm will be thrilled by the multitude of small species that are drawn to the sandy terraces or branches of gorgonians and corals (gobies, symbiont shrimps and nudibranchs). Divers who want to test their luck will have to venture about 30 meters away from the wall, keeping it just barely in sight, and proceed horizontally as far as possible, methodically examining the blue-green depths that yawn toward the open water. At 20-40 meters they are likely to see grey reef sharks, *Carcharhinus amblyrhynchos* or, more rarely, the giant mantas, *Manta birostris*, and scalloped hammerhead sharks, *Sphyrna lewini*. Unfortunately, most of the time the frenetic movements of less experienced divers and the blasts of compressed air horns may reduce the encounter to only a few seconds. It may be a selfish suggestion, but if you are lucky enough to be the first to make such a sighting, it is often advisable to discreetly alert only your diving companion and try to enjoy the spectacle offered by these great creatures as long as possible, without alerting the entire group. These circumstances often trigger an unseemly lack of self-control in some divers, who appear to believe that the best way to observe a large creature is by frantically swimming toward it while sounding a noisy compressed air horn. At greater depths, if divers are very lucky, they may spot a rare fox shark, *Alopias vulpinus*, and at the end of the dive, on the shallow seabeds, they are liable to find themselves in the middle of a large vortex of bigeye trevallies or barracuda. These move methodically along the perimeter of the island, and are sometimes accompanied by a large leopard shark, *Stegostoma fasciatum*, returning from the depths in the late afternoon.

G

H

E

F

E - Fire dartfish, Nemateleotris magnifica, *generally live in pairs at depths of between five and 50 meters. You may see one hovering above its lair dug in the substratum, into which it will make a rapid retreat if you come too close.*

F - Nudibranchs *from the genus* Chromodoris *are notable for their elegant forms and colors. The specimen pictured is from the species* Chromodoris willani.

G - Between 10 and 40 meters deep, the submerged cavities and balconies of Staghorn Crest are an ideal habitat for the majestic striped angelfish, Pomacanthus sexstriatus.

H - Generally hidden among the corals during the day, the striped cleaner fish, Stenopus hispidus, comes out of hiding at night.

HANGING GARDENS

INDIA

THE PHILIPPINES

PACIFIC OCEAN

N

MALAYSIA

BORNEO

SIPADAN

PAPUA NEW GUINEA

INDONESIA

INDIAN OCEAN

AUSTRALIA

0 m

18 m

25 m

50 m

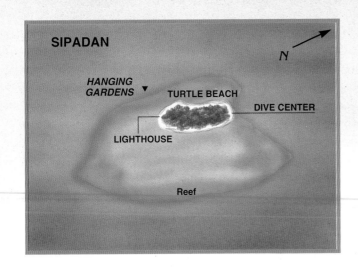

SIPADAN

HANGING GARDENS ▼

TURTLE BEACH

DIVE CENTER

LIGHTHOUSE

Reef

N

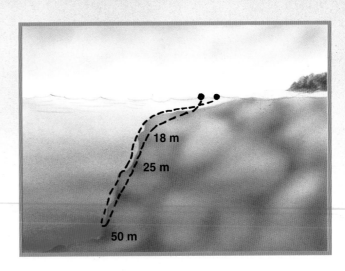

18 m

25 m

50 m

This classical wall dive is almost entirely along a vertical drop-off which begins just a little over a meter from the surface, then descends to a sandy terrace at a depth of about 70 meters. From here the seabed rapidly plunges into the abyss. The dive always follows the flow of the current, which is rarely strong here.

By keeping the wall to their left divers will inevitably be picked up by the support boat near Lobster Lairs, which is the adjacent diving site. If they keep the wall to their right, they can try to reach the drop-off by passing West Ridge, then conclude the dive directly on the beach (but they must be

C

A - The wall of Hanging Gardens is extraordinarily full of sessile organisms, including fan gorgonians, colonies of black corals, hard corals and large alcyonarians of every shape and color, making this seascape exceptionally spectacular.

B - Particularly numerous on the jutting vaults of Hanging Gardens are the alcyonarians from the genus Dendronephthya, which swell to maximum size when the current sweeps along the wall.

C - On the deeper seabeds, divers are treated to the sight of whip gorgonians from the genus Elisella. Little gobies, Bryaninops loki, can be observed among their scarlet branches.

D - Sea turtles, which have become the symbol of Sipadan, are common in these waters. Pictured is an enormous old male turtle from the genus Chelonia mydas, heading toward the open water.

A

D

B

careful not to overestimate their strength!)

The name of the site is due to the large festoons of *Dendronephythya alcyonarians* in delicate pastel hues - lemon, lavender and antique rose - which adorn the projecting vaults and are at their most splendid when, swollen by the current, they protrude in search of nourishment. Despite their beauty, the alcyonarians of Sipadan do not compare with those of the Red Sea or the Fiji islands. It is better for photographers to concentrate on the microfauna that nests in them and populates the gigantic gorgonians in the genera *Subergorgia* and *Siphonogorgia*

and the enormous colonies of black corals in the genus *Antipatharia* which adorn this wall.

Don't forget to explore the cavities and crevices that open in the wall, populated by colonies of *Plectorynchus* sweetlips, pairs of *Pomacanthus imperator* and *xanthometopon* emperor angelfish, and large tropical groupers from the genus *Cephalopholis*.

With its multitude of species, Hanging Gardens can pose a few problems in choosing which lenses to take down on a dive there. Large species such as green turtles, *Chelonia mydas*, and imbricate turtles, *Eretmochelys*

E - A tiny, bright yellow damselfish, Amblyglyphodon aureus, *is silhouetted on a colony of sponges.*

F - The top reef of Hanging Gardens offers an extraordinarily rich and complex panorama, a typical example of a tropical coral reef in perfect health.

G - At Hanging Gardens at a depth of between two and forty meters, you are likely to encounter the spectacular yellowmask angelfish, Pomacanthus xanthometapon.

H - If you explore the corals that dot the sandy terraces of Hanging Gardens, it is not difficult to spot a blue-spotted ribbontail reef stingray, Taeniura lymma.

I - This once-in-a-lifetime encounter is also an unforgettable photo opportunity. Fox sharks, Alopias superciliusus *(the specimen photographed, however, is difficult to identify and could belong to the species* pelagicus*), exlusively frequent the open sea and deep waters.*

imbricata, are quite common, as are blue-spotted ribbontail stingrays, *Taeniura lymma*, resting on the terraces, but it is just as common to see exotic, brightly colored nudibranchs (*Chromodoris, Casella, Phyllidia* and *Nembrotha*), tiny gobies residing in the gorgonians, hawkfish, *Oxycirrhites typus*, hidden in the coral, and rare morays peeping out of their lairs. Finally, there is the ever-present possibility, here more than anywhere else, of sensational encounters with large predators. Indeed, in deep water it is common to see grey reef sharks, *Carcharhinus amblyrhynchos*, leopard sharks, *Stegostoma*

E

fasciatum, and single specimens or even a gigantic sedentary school of scalloped hammerhead sharks, *Sphyrna lewini*.
If you are especially lucky, you may get a glimpse of the rare fox sharks, *Alopias superciliosus* and *vulpinus*, pelagic predators characterized by the unmistakable and spectacular development of the caudal fin.

F

G

H

I

PULAU MABUL & KAPALAI

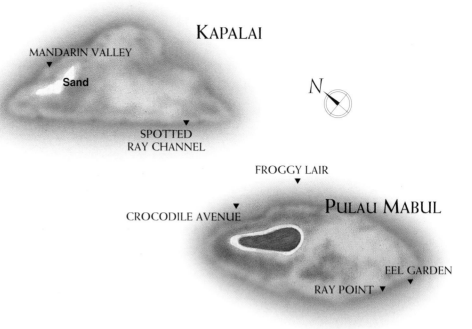

KAPALAI

MANDARIN VALLEY
▼
Sand

SPOTTED
RAY CHANNEL ▼

N

FROGGY LAIR
▼

CROCODILE AVENUE ▼

PULAU MABUL

EEL GARDEN
▼

RAY POINT ▼

Although Sipadan's seabeds are still some of the most rich and beautiful in the world, the island has inevitably suffered from overcrowding in recent years due to its fame and the rampant proliferation of tourist structures on its very limited surface area. Those who saw Sipadan five or six years ago cannot help but notice signs of deterioration (especially in the atmosphere) due solely to human impact.

A

B

Divers looking for a rustic, relaxed atmosphere similar to Sipadan as it once was, would do well to stay at Pulau Mabul, a small, sandy island a little larger than Sipadan which is less than half an hour's sail from its more famous sister. This is particularly so if they are interested in microfauna that is extremely rare and hard to find at other sites.

Closer to the mainland, Mabul does not offer the steep walls that have made Sipadan famous, and unlike Sipadan, its history has deprived it of its original cloak of forests. One quarter of its beaches is occupied by a rather dilapidated *kampung* (village) of Filipino fishermen who immigrated semi-legally, and is entirely covered by a plantation of coconut palms, which makes it look a bit like certain Maldivian postcard islands. There are two resorts on Mabul: the elegant Water Village, jutting out onto the reef with its pilework bungalows, and the tranquil Sipadan-Mabul Resort (known as SMART), which is more discreet and hidden among the palms. With few exceptions, the seabeds are decidedly mediocre, at least from the perspective of coral formations. Diving sites are almost all at ridiculously shallow depths (from 2 to 20 meters), often on sandy, muddy or even detrital seabeds. The nearby sandbank of Kapalai, which emerges only during low tide, offers quite similar seabeds.

In recent years, various areas of the reef have suffered massive devastation through the practice of dynamite fishing, and dives are accompanied by sharp explosions with almost clockwork regularity, despite government prohibitions and regular patrols by government boats (there is also a police station on Mabul). Local fishermen also contribute to the impoverishment of marine fauna in the surrounding waters, by fishing with nets along the deep channels that divide the island from Sipadan and the coast in a continuous search for sharks to supply the lucrative, Oriental market for shark fins. It is not infrequent to see the small outrigger canoes used by locals returning loaded with silky sharks, and the occasional tiger shark.

If the picture looks bleak at first, here's the surprise: Mabul is actually an extraordinary paradise for an equally extraordinary variety of rare and spectacular species which are quite difficult to observe during normal dives. These species have extremely specialized behaviors and ecological niches and are highly sought after by photographers who appreciate macro-photography, and more in general by all divers who have learned to appreciate and admire the eccentric, the bizarre, the curious, and even the monstrous. Mabul is still a "secret" destination reserved for a very few, and it is no accident that the great majority of divers who come to this area, unaware of its treasures, decide to dive at Sipadan. Above all, Mabul is the other aspect of this sea, its third facet - perfectly complementary to the oceanic seabeds of Layang Layang and the teeming, multicolored walls of Sipadan. No connoisseur of the seas of Borneo could consider his explorations complete without a dive on its seabeds.

Every dive holds a surprise or a new species, always rare or at least uncommon, always strange, and always difficult to identify without the aid of the by now highly expert local dive masters, who have truly invented a professional specialization. In the "muck dives" of Mabul, the extraordinary becomes ordinary, and the dense, suspended particles that permanently cloud the underwater horizons transform into a mysterious curtain behind which long sought-after creatures hide, in which the horrifying and wondrous live side by side and merge. Mabul, whose evening skies witness the passage of

C

D

flying foxes, and along whose beaches sea snakes, *Laticauda colubrina*, crawl under the moonlight, is the underwater kingdom of ghost pipefish, *Solenostomus cyanopterus* and *paradoxus*, devil scorpionfish, *Scorpaenopsis* and *Inimicus*, *Synanceia* stonefish, *Odontodactylus* mantis shrimps, mandarin fish, *Synchiropus splendidus* and *picturatus*, ribbon eels, *Rhynomuraena quaesita*, snake eels, frogfish, sea horses and crocodile fish - an extraordinary bestiary of eighteenth century monstrosities that seem to belong to the world of fantasy rather than reality.

A - An aerial photo of Pulau Mabul shows the satellite reef of Kapalai in the distance.

B - During low tide, Mabul can be reached by a long pier.

C - Despite the murky water, the coral gardens of Mabul boast a wide variety of species.

D - The sandy clearings among the coral formations often offer the chance to approach splendid specimens of

turtles, from the genus Chelonia mydas.

E - The absence of large predators on the reefs of Mabul and Kapalai makes it possible to spot fascinating mollusks such as this large octopus, Octopus cyaneus

F - There are a great many scorpionfish on these seabeds. The most common and colorful is probably the tasseled scorpionfish, Scorpaenopsis oxycephala.

E

F

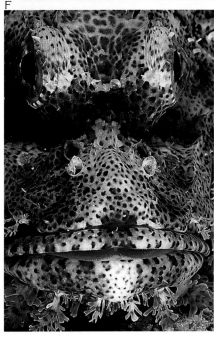

MANDARIN VALLEY

INDIA

THE PHILIPPINES

PACIFIC OCEAN

N

MALAYSIA

KAPALAI

BORNEO

PAPUA NEW GUINEA

INDONESIA

INDIAN OCEAN

AUSTRALIA

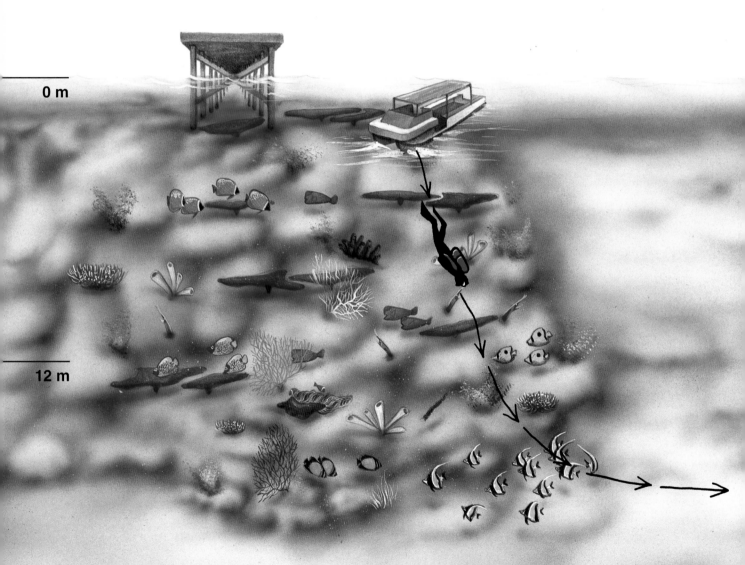

0 m

12 m

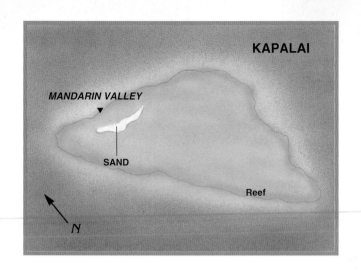

KAPALAI

MANDARIN VALLEY

SAND

Reef

N

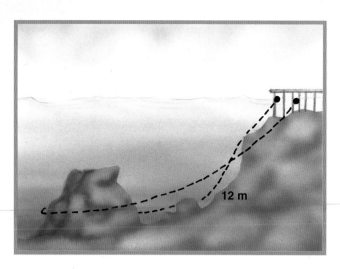

12 m

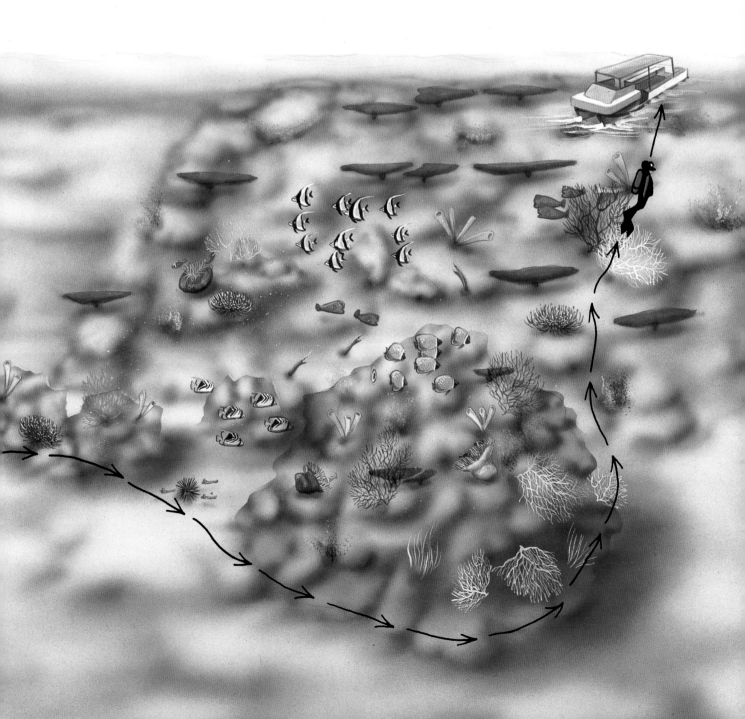

Easily accessible by just a few minutes' sail from Pulau Mabul, Pulau Kapalai is actually not a true island, but a simple sandbank. Its summit, on which a long wooden pier has been built, emerges only at low tide.

Although the devastating and illegal practice of dynamite fishing has heavily damaged the coral reef that surrounds Kapalai in many areas, such as Gurnard Ground, the reef nevertheless offers easy and quite exciting dives. One of these is in Mandarin Valley, a site with a depth that varies from eight to 20 meters.

Divers begin on a gentle coral slope that they should keep to

A

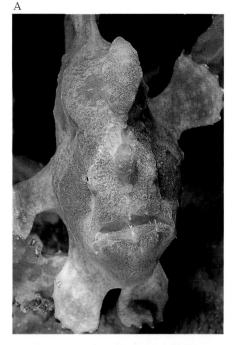

B

C

their left. Among the coral formations and sandy terraces that characterize the area, they will see large stonefish, *Synanceia verrucosa*, rare frogfish perfectly camouflaged on the candelabra sponges, young isolated specimens of giant parrotfish, *Bolbometopon muricatum*, and many other examples of fauna which, if present, indicate a healthy coral reef. Careful observation of the seabed will also yield several large tropical cuttlefish, *Sepia pharaonis*, sheltered among the corals, or, much smaller but disguised with equal skill, a ghost pipefish, *Solenostomus cyanopterus*, busily engaged in

D

looking like a leaf of Neptune seagrass. Crossing a wide sandy gully, traveled by the large sharks which patrol the surrounding deep waters at night, divers will come to a broad rocky area emerging from the sandy substratum, entirely covered by a multitude of sessile organisms - gorgonians, soft corals, anemones and sponges in every color, shape and sizes. Hidden within the fissures of the rocks among the fragments of dead coral and the impenetrable, intricate structure of the long spines of the *Diadema* sea urchins, circle beautiful, unapproachable mandarinfish, *Synchiropus splendidus* and *Synchiropus picturatus*, tiny and

A - Very difficult to spot, the frogfish Antennarius moluccensis is a sedentary predator with extraordinary mimetic skills.

B - The brightly colored mantle of a common large bivalve, Spondylus aurantius, adds a bright touch of color to the walls of the Malaysian seas.

C . Rare elsewhere, the blue ribbon eel, Rhinomuraena quaesita, is common at shallow depths in various diving sites at Mabul and Kapalai.

D - Whip gorgonians from the genus Juncella generally prefer deep water. At Mabul they can be seen only a few meters deep, along with the gobies and crustaceans which normally live in them.

E - Tiny but vividly colored, gobies from the genus Eviota permanently occupy well-defined territories on formations of corals from the genera Favia and Turbinaria.

F - This rare sea snail is camouflaged on a coral.

G - On the more exposed areas of the reef, it is not difficult to observe crinoids from the genus Comanthina.

H - The leaf scorpionfish, Taenianotus triacanthus, has various color phases: white, brown, green, red and yellow.

I - The Chromodoris bullocki nudibranch is one of the showiest inhabitants of the reef.

brilliantly colored. The same habitat is shared by equally spectacular nocturnal crayfish from the genus *Saron*, which can sometimes be glimpsed in the darker crevices.
All around are extremely beautiful nudibranchs, brightly colored rare flatworms, various species of scorpionfish, including the leaf scorpionfish, *Taenianotus triacanthus*, with its unusual deep yellow color, pipefish, large schools of cardinalfish, and cleaner shrimp from the genera *Periclemenes*, *Lysmata* and *Stenopus*.
In great numbers everywhere, resting on the sandy substratum or lying in wait on the cupules of

Porites coral, are large lizardfish, *Synodus variegatus*, blennies, gobies, Moorish idols, *Zanclus cornutus*, glittering blue ribbon eels, *Rhinomuraena quaesita*, and butterflyfish from the genus *Chaetodon*.
Mandarin Valley is truly a paradise for underwater photographers and those interested in small, rare species. The weak current that flows through more or less continuously usually guarantees excellent visibility, and the shallow average depth of the dive (about 10 meters) permits divers with a degree of experience to stay under for long periods of time.

F

G

H

I

SPOTTED RAY CHANNEL

INDIA

THE PHILIPPINES

PACIFIC OCEAN

MALAYSIA

KAPALAI

BORNEO

PAPUA NEW GUINEA

INDIAN OCEAN

INDONESIA

AUSTRALIA

N

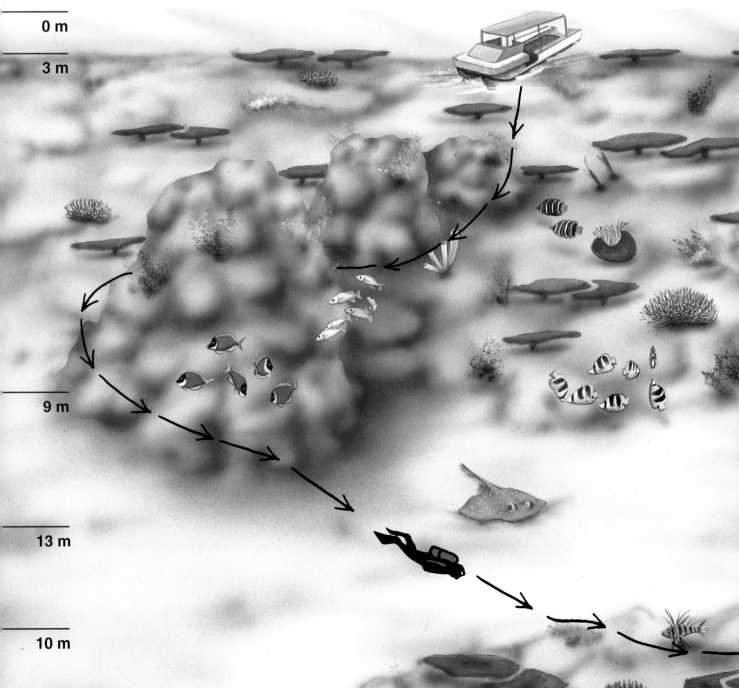

0 m

3 m

9 m

13 m

10 m

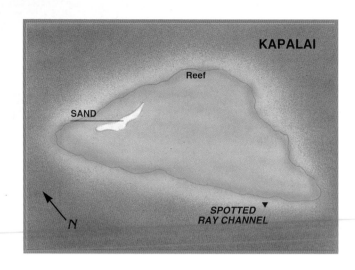

KAPALAI

Reef

SAND

SPOTTED
RAY CHANNEL

N

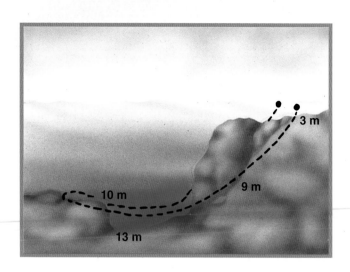

3 m

9 m

10 m

13 m

A

B

C

T he diving site known as
Spotted Ray Channel is
located at the southern tip of the
Kapalai sandbank.
Although it is exactly opposite
Mandarin Valley, it is actually
quite similar to it. Here as well,
the dive begins on a gently
descending coral slope with great
biological diversity, with an initial
stop devoted to an examination
of the large round rock several
meters in size which stands on
the sandy substratum at the base
of the reef. The dive also
continues by crossing a wide,
sandy gully to finally reach a
series of rocky outcrops entirely
covered with coral, situated
parallel to the Kapalai reef at a

D

depth of about 15 meters.
On the large rock that greets
divers at the beginning of the
dive, or in its immediate vicinity,
are various members of the
scorpionfish family: leaf
scorpionfish, *Taenianotus
triacanthus*, reef scorpionfish,
Scorpaenopsis venosa and
oxycephala, large specimens of
stonefish, *Synanceia verrucosa*,
perfectly camouflaged among the
coral fragments, and various
species of *Pterois* turkeyfish.
Here and there the lovely blue
ribbon eels, *Rhinomuraena
quaesita*, nervously peep out
of their lairs, while, nearly
invisible, a delicately lavender-
colored frogfish, *Antennarius*

*A - Due to its
exposure to the
current, visibility
on the reef of
Kapalai is often
good. Pictured
is a coral block
colonized by some
of the most
extraordinary forms
of underwater life.*

*B - The tangle of
Acropora colonies
on the top reef offers
refuge for a myriad
of the brightly
colored young of
various species.*

*C - An absolute
master in the
difficult art of
camouflage,
Octopus cyaneus
can instantly
change its shape
and color.*

*D - If you explore
the areas shaded
by the corals, you
are likely to observe
an elegant blue-
spotted ribbontail
reef stingray,
Taeniura lymma.*

pictus, comfortably grasps the branches of a candelabra sponge of the same color as it waits patiently for a careless prey.

As divers cross the wide sandy gully that separatesthem from the parallel reef, they cannot help but disturb a myriad of gobies, ready to dart back into their tunnels along with their co-tenants, *Alpheus* shrimp, and perhaps a few spotted rays from the species *Taeniura lymma* or *Dasyatis kuhlii*.

When they finally come to the submerged reefs that await them on their right, they will find an underwater garden of extraordinary richness and beauty. Here is an infinite number

E

G

E - Another extraordinary example of mimetic skill is demonstrated by the stonefish, *Synanceia verrucosa, which with its poisonous spines is one of the most dangerous creatures in the tropical seas.*

F - The ability to change color means survival at Mabul and Kapalai. This splendid frogfish, *Antennarius moluccensis, is nearly indistinguishable from the sponge on which it rests.*

G - Here is another astounding example of mimicry, offered by a tiny ghost pipefish, *Solenostomus cyanopterus. It looks exactly like an algae-encrusted leaf of Potomogetonaceae.*

H - First impressions notwithstanding, even Mabul and Kapalai are quite colorful. The photo shows a tiny bristlestar which has found shelter among the corals.

F

of interesting sights: beautiful, rare nudibranchs and flatworms, shrimp of every species and size, sea anemones with symbiotic clownfish, and crabs, blennies, gobies, sponges and corals of various species.

With a bit of luck and a lot of observation, divers may also approach a fascinating and timid resident of these seabeds, the tropical octopus, *Octopus cyaneus*, which is difficult to find in tropical seas due to predation by large morays and groupers. Evidently the coral garden of Spotted Ray Channel at Kapalai cannot boast great populations of either of the latter, because here it is rather easy to spot

Octopus cynaeus, even during the day (tropical octopuses are almost exclusively nocturnal, to avoid predators). More than almost any other marine animal, octopuses and cuttlefish give those who observe and respect them the extraordinary impression of surprising, speculative intelligence.

Once divers have ended their exploration of the submerged reef, they return across the sandy gully to their left and conclude the dive with a safety stop, suspended over the Kapalai reef.

H

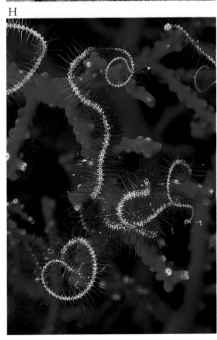

EEL GARDEN

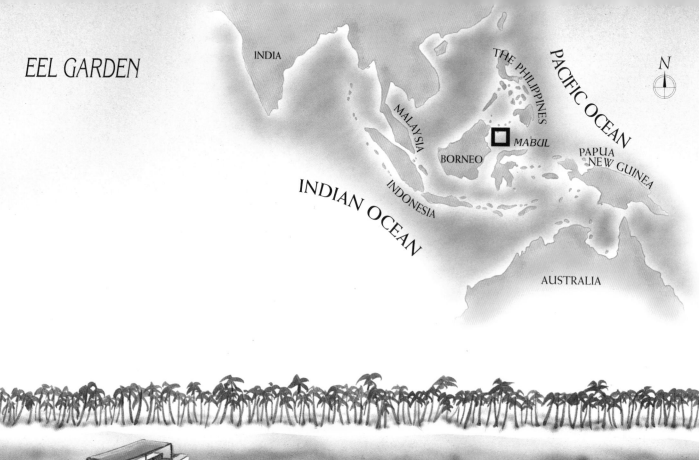

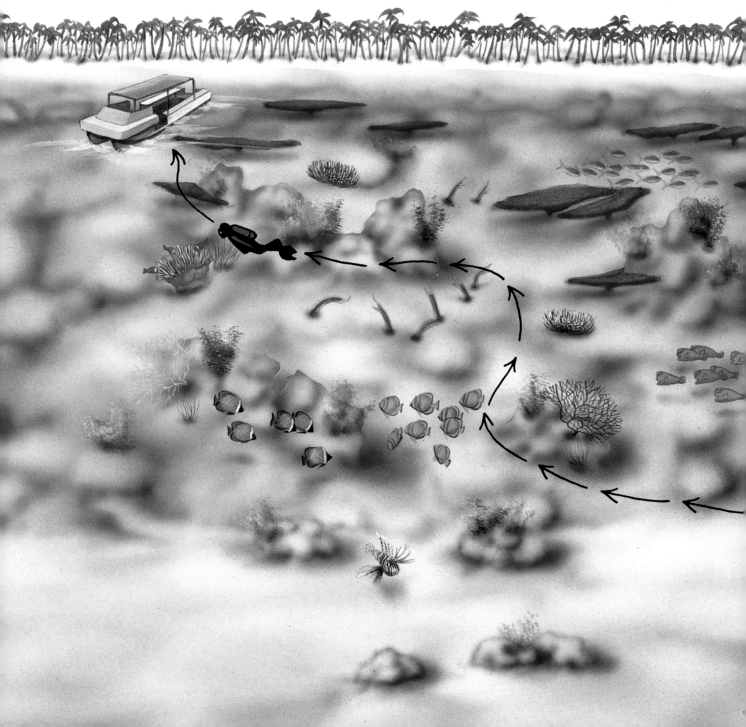

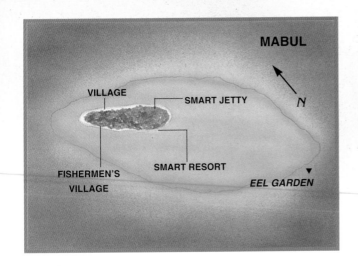

MABUL

VILLAGE

SMART JETTY

FISHERMEN'S VILLAGE

SMART RESORT

EEL GARDEN

N

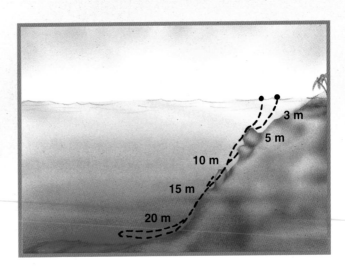

3 m

5 m

10 m

15 m

20 m

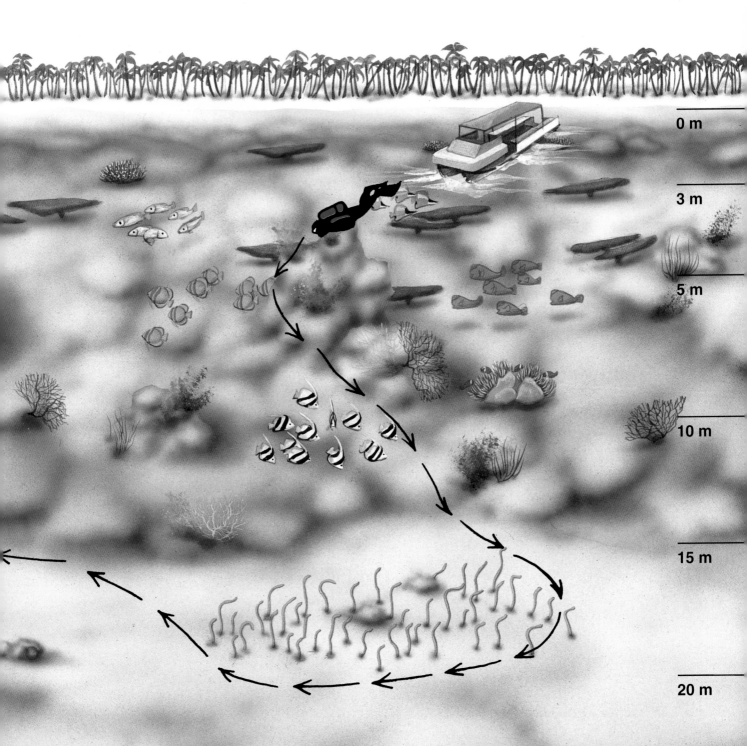

0 m

3 m

5 m

10 m

15 m

20 m

A

B

C

D

L ocated at the southernmost tip of the reef that surrounds the island of Mabul, of all the sites discussed in this section, Eel Garden is where divers can reach the greatest depth, about 25 meters. Actually, Pulau Mabul has a true vertical drop-off known as Lobster Wall, which exceeds a depth of 40 meters, but as the most characteristic and interesting discoveries can be made at much shallower depths, we have decided not to discuss it as a diving area in

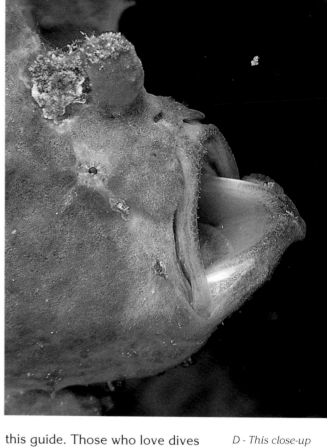

E

this guide. Those who love dives on walls will find nothing different here, either by day or night, than what they can see at Sipadan. Divers at Eel Garden will immediately come to a sandy flat area at a depth ranging from 20-26 meters, which juts out from the base of the reef into the open waters, with its outer limit interrupted by a few small, isolated coral formations. Here, carefully observing the sandy seabed and moving very cautiously to avoid raising clouds

A - The top reef of Eel Garden is populated by a surprising variety of species.

B - The lamellar formations of Turbinaria coral are characteristic of shallow depths.

C - If you swim calmly, you can approach even timid creatures like the blue ribbon eel, Rhynomuraena quaesita.

D - This close-up of a Rhynomuraena quaesita *shows the flashing yellow and electric blue colors of adults of the species.*

E - This close-up of a frogfish, Antennarius moluccensis, *reveals the wide jaws of this skillfully camouflaged predator.*

F - By carefully observing the sandy and detrital substratum it will not be difficult to spot the snout of a lizardfish from the genus Synodus *as it lies in wait.*

G - The seabeds of Mabul and Kapalai offer the opportunity to observe the brilliant colors of the peacock mantis shrimp, Odontodactylus scyllaris, *an extremely active predator.*

of suspended particles, they will see a multitude of small lairs and tunnels that open into the sandy substratum, from which numerous brightly colored gobies of various species, some rare, peep cautiously out, always accompanied by the indefatigable shrimp from the genus *Alpheus*, obsessively cleaning the entrance of their burrows.

By controlling breathing and keeping movement to a minimum, patient divers will be able to get a

H

F

G

I

The ascent will gradually follow the line of the reef, which is more luxuriant here than in other areas of Mabul (the almost constant current also guarantees better visibility here).

Among the sights which are uncommon elsewhere are frogfish, perfectly camouflaged on the sponges at about 18 meters. They are generally lavender, antique rose or deep black in color. This creature is extremely interesting because of its prehensile fins/paws (which have also given it its name) and the deceptive apparatus (the decoy and *illicium*) that protrudes from the front of its head like a little worm. It is used to attract unsuspecting prey to this predator's cavernous mouth.

On the sandy terraces and in the detrital substratum, it is also easy to spot the rare and extremely beautiful blue ribbon eel, *Rhinomuraena quaesita*, which peeps out from its lair in spasmodic and apparently disorganized movements. Adults are a deep electric blue with

H - This leaf scorpionfish, Taenianotus triacanthus, *was photographed during its brown color phase. Note the lighter marks that simulate algae concretions.*

I - The pixy hawkfish, Cirrhitichthys oxycephalus, *is a small, active predator at shallow and medium depths, and is quite attracted to corals.*

close-up view of the fascinating "condominium" life of the little creatures that live here, while all around the numerous garden eels that give this site its name oscillate in the gentle current, like miniature periscopes peeping out from the sandy seabed.

Don't forget to explore the small coral masses, which are used as cleaning stations by groups of elegant shrimp from the genus *Periclemenes* or as a lair for the rare lemon-colored moray, *Gymnothorax fimbriatus.*

touches of bright yellow on the snout, while immature individuals are velvety black edged with chrome yellow.

Along the reef at depths ranging from two to 15 meters are other interesting specimens.

Watch out for the holes in the sandy floor.

As large as a man's wrist, they may appear to be the tips of the membranous tubes of the *Cerianthus*, but they actually hide the gigantic mantis shrimp from the genus *Odontodactylus*, a formidable predatory crustacean about 40 centimeters long.

When cautiously approached, it can be seen coming out of its lair, observing everything around it with its pedunculate eyes. If a potential prey, such as a wrasse or a damselfish, passes above its den, in a fraction of a second the mantis shrimp leaps upward, grabbing the fish in the deadly grip of its front claws, and violently withdraws with it back into its lair. Not infrequently the violence of the impact breaks the unfortunate fish in two. Indeed, the force of the attack has been compared to a 22-caliber bullet. These crustaceans have been nicknamed "thumb-splitters" by fishermen for good reason. Some species have clawed raptorial paws, while others have a hammer form capable of crushing the shells of the crabs

C

A

B

D

A - The relative transparency of the waters permits a vigorous growth of the top reef at Eel Garden.

B - A careful examination of the base of the coral formations reveals the lair of a rare barred fin moray, Gymnothorax zonipectis.

C - A diver observes a block of coral entirely colonized by green Acropora.

D - The corals at Eel Garden often hide immature pinnate batfish, Platax pinnatus, characterized by their unmistakable orange-edged scales.

E - The photographer's lens shows the particularly bright colors of this starfish.

F - A wrasse (probably from the genus Cheilinus*) hides among the fronds of a soft coral.*

G - This immature clown anemonefish, Amphiprion ocellaris, *peers out from the tentacles of the anemone that hosts it.*

H - One of the most common morays on the reefs of Mabul and Kapalai is the small white-eyed moray, Siderea thyrsoidea, *which is quite active during the day.*

I - Nudibranchs with brilliant and variegated colors can be observed on the seabeds of Mabul and Kapalai.

on which they feed.
The diver, however, has nothing to worry about if he avoids provoking them (although the temptation to goad them into action by offering them pieces of fish is great).
Eel Garden also boasts many brightly colored nudibranchs, many of which are unusually large and some of which are quite rare; small, odd-looking, white-eyed morays, *Siderea thyrsoidea*; crocodile fish, *Cymbacephalus beauforti*; gigantic parrotfish, *Bolbometopon muricatum*; and various scorpionfish.
One of the many exclusive characteristics of dives at Mabul is the chance for close-range

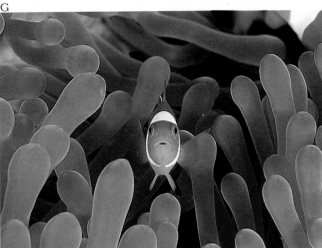

observation of great quantities of immature individuals, which evidently find this area a safe and adequately protected refuge. In Eel Garden divers are likely to see spectacular immature specimens of batfish, *Platax pinnatus*, extremely elegant with their black scales edged in bright orange; small *Pterois radiata*, or clearfin turkeyfish, just a few months old, more similar to animated jewels than to turkeyfish; numerous newborn clown anemonefish, guests of the large anemones in the company of adults of the same species; cleaner shrimp from the genus *Periclemenes* and the splendid *Neopetrolisthes* crabs.

RAY POINT

INDIA

THE PHILIPPINES

PACIFIC OCEAN

MALAYSIA

☐ MABUL

BORNEO

PAPUA NEW GUINEA

INDIAN OCEAN

INDONESIA

AUSTRALIA

N

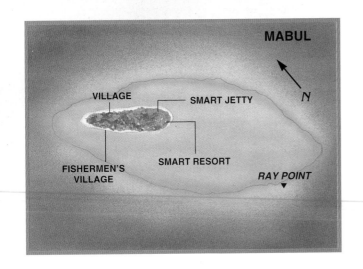

MABUL

VILLAGE

SMART JETTY

SMART RESORT

FISHERMEN'S
VILLAGE

RAY POINT

N

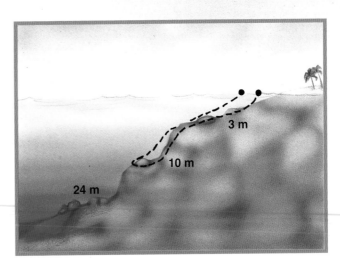

3 m

10 m

24 m

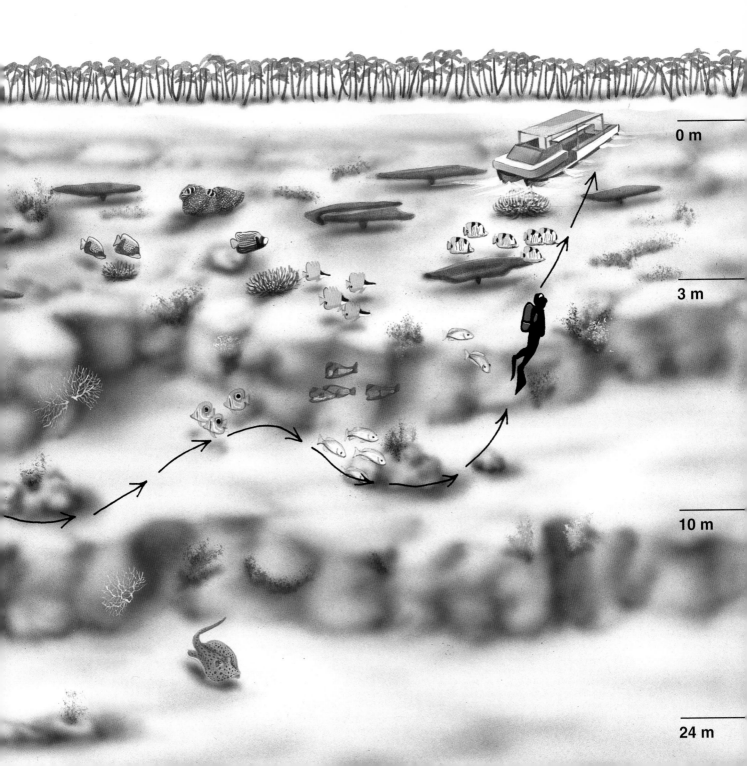

0 m

3 m

10 m

24 m

A dive at Ray Point is rather different from the typically flat, shallow diving that characterizes the seabeds of Pulau Mabul and the nearby sandbank of Pulau Kapalai. Here, in fact, the reef slopes down toward the sandy seabed at a depth of about 25-30 meters, with a pleasantly disorganized succession of sandy steps and coral terraces. In the crevices of these can be spotted some very interesting creatures.
Like Eel Garden, the closest diving site, Ray Point is located on the southern tip of the reef of Pulau Mabul, and is often affected by weak currents which make the visibility quite good. The greater clarity of the water and the

B

A

C

A - The crevices of the reef reveal a colony of serpula worms, probably from the genus Filogranella.

B - It is possible to see numerous fans of perfectly developed gorgonians along the slope explored during this dive.

nutritional substances brought in by the currents result in particularly luxuriant coral and top reef formations. The top reef reached at the end of the dive is a garden of rich, multicolored corals that rivals similar locations at Sipadan and Layang Layang, with the greater diversity of species characteristic of the coral reef. There are particularly large numbers of butterflyfish, angelfish, emperors, damselfish, parrotfish (especially the large group of *Bolbometopon muricatum*) and all the brightly colored species usually seen in the maze of corals which form tropical reefs.

Along the "step" that leads gradually to the sandy seabed, it is possible to come across some more unusual sights: upon closer observation, a stalk of Neptune seagrass leaf drifting delicately in the current reveals a ghost pipefish, *Solenostomus paradoxus* or *cyanopterus*, with its extraordinary camouflage; a coral fragment no larger than a thumbnail may transform malevolently before your eyes into an immature false stonefish, *Scorpaenopsis diabolus*; and a fragment of clear algae, corroded by the sea and oscillating gently, may betray the cold, opalescent glare of a

C - The top reef of Ray Point is adorned with a rich coral garden.

D - Rather rare elsewhere, the elegant spotted-face moray, *Gymnothorax fimbriatus*, is easy to find on the seabeds of Mabul and Kapalai.

leaf scorpionfish, *Taenianotus triacanthus*. Lying in wait on the sandy terraces, perfectly camouflaged in the detrital substratum in the shade of the corals, are large crocodile fish, *Cymbacephalus beauforti*, blue-spotted ribbontail reef stingrays, *Taeniura lymma*, large common scorpionfish, *Scorpaenopsis venosa* and *barbata*, tiny, colorful dragonets *Synchiropus ocellatus*, ringed pipefish, *Doryrhamphus dactyliophorus*, and large stonefish, *Synanceia verrucosa*. The latter have an appearance that accurately reflects their true danger to careless divers, who may be injured by the extremely poisonous rays of their dorsal fins. The parallel kingdom of the miniscule reveals other unusual wonders at Ray Point: nudibranchs of every species and color, especially *Chromodoris* and *Phyllidia*, which crawl through the sand, flatworms similar to sinuous, sumptuous Oriental cloth, and ghost crabs and their fellow shrimp that peep out warily from among the pearly "bubbles" of *Pleurogyra sinuosa* corals. Spend the safety stop at the end of the dive suspended on the top reef in the company of schools of anthias and butterflyfish.

D

E

F

E - Large crocodile fish, Cymbacephalus beauforti, *perfectly camouflaged on the detrital seabed, can be seen on the sandy terraces and balconies of Ray Point.*

F - Lying in wait among the rocks on the sea floor, a large stonefish, Synanceia verrucosa, *covered with algae, waits motionless for its unsuspecting prey. Because there are numerous individuals of this species here, it is not advisable to stand on the reefs of Kapalai and Mabul.*

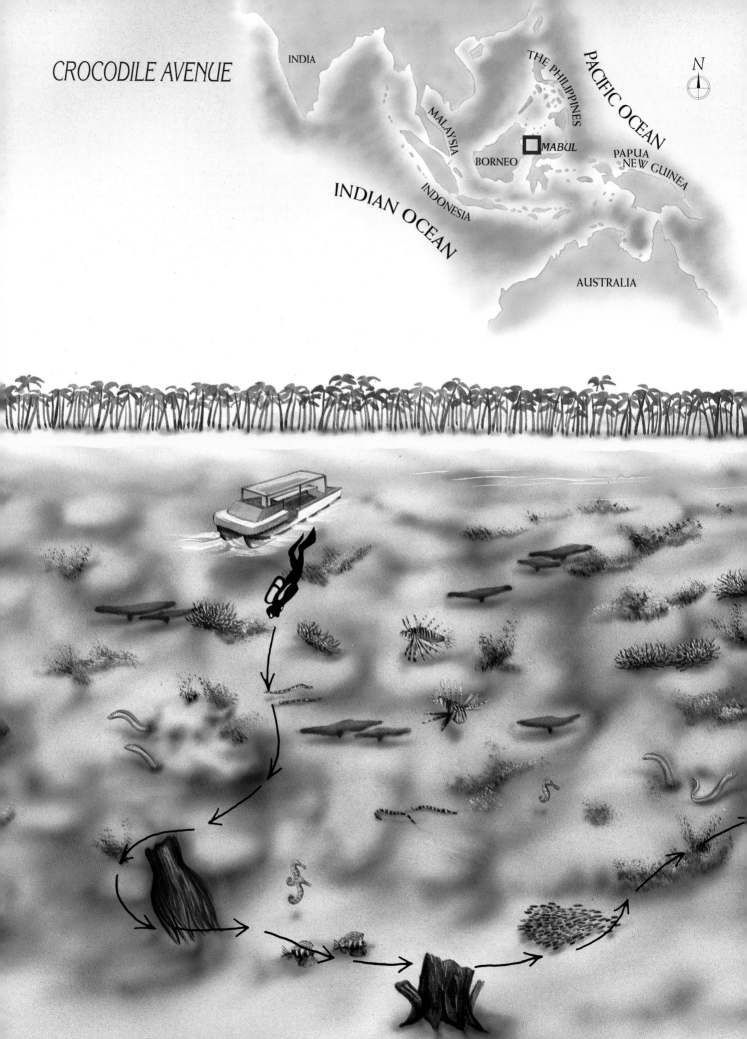

CROCODILE AVENUE

INDIA

MALAYSIA

THE PHILIPPINES

PACIFIC OCEAN

BORNEO

MABUL

PAPUA
NEW GUINEA

INDONESIA

INDIAN OCEAN

AUSTRALIA

N

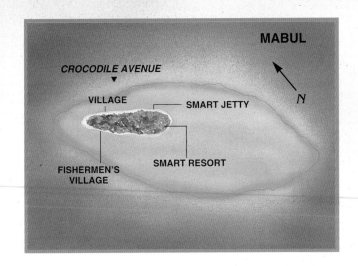

MABUL

CROCODILE AVENUE ▾

VILLAGE

SMART JETTY

FISHERMEN'S
VILLAGE

SMART RESORT

N

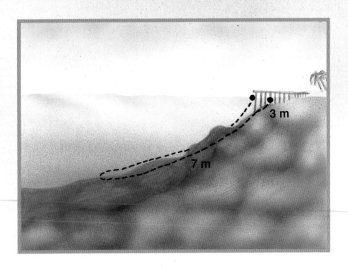

3 m

7 m

0 m

3 m

7 m

A

B

C

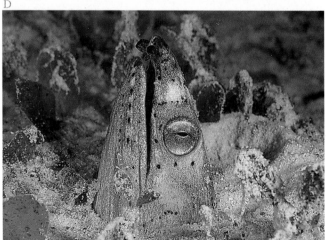

D

At first sight, few seabeds seems as disheartening as Crocodile Avenue. Located at the far northern tip of the reef that surrounds Pulau Mabul, at a depth that varies from two to 15 meters, the sight that greets divers as they first enter the water seems almost lunar - a stretch of coarse sand and mud that extends uniformly in all directions, immersed in an opaline, milky luminosity caused by fine, suspended particles that limit visibility to no more than five or six meters.

The only sign of life is the uniform network of green algae with small, round, fleshy leaves

E

stretching out across the seabed. Here and there, vague shadows appear in the dim light and materialize after a few cautious fin strokes: the indestructible radical stump of a large coconut palm, now resting on the mud of the seabed, a vestige of the floorboards of an old canoe sunk countless years ago. A large palm leaf once used as a rudimentary stretcher for a fishing boat is weighed down on one side by an old rusty drum half-buried in the sand, and waves softly up toward the surface. A few ropes tied in large knots rise up from the seabed, suspended to a buoy utilized as a mooring.
But experts and veterans know

A - An immature crocodile fish, Cymbacephalus beauforti, *slides peacefully on the sand, sure of its perfect camouflage.*

B - At Crocodile Avenue it is not uncommon to come across "steamroller" schools of young striped catfish, Plotosus lineatus, *armed with poisonous spines.*

C - A tiny crab, perhaps from the genus Calappa, *hides among the grains of sand on the seabed.*

D - A rare and fascinating encounter: poking out of the muddy substratum is the snout of an unidentified snake eel, probably from the genus Myrichthys.

E - Crocodile Avenue is full of fascinating discoveries such as this sea horse, Hippocampus histrix, *which has now become rare elsewhere in Southeast Asia due to overfishing.*

what awaits them. Crocodile Avenue is the classical "muck dive", over 90 minutes long. If the diver suspends himself just a few centimeters over the shapeless seabed, head down and feet up, and maintains his position through breath control, he will already be able to see the first fascinating results of his search. There are two ways of exploring: either a methodical examination of the seabed, or a careful check of the above-noted submerged plant fragments, which are a center of attraction for many members of the local microfauna. Either technique, both of which are pleasant and relaxing, will lead to many interesting

F

G

H
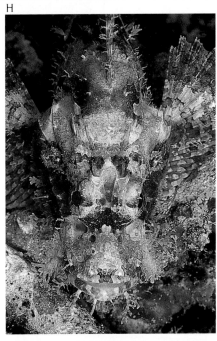

I

F - An encounter with the extraordinary, tiny harlequin ghost pipefish, Solenostomus paradoxus, *is one of the most sought-after by underwater photographers.*

G - The sandy seabeds are the kingdom of soles and flounder, like this curious unidentified member of the Bothus *genus.*

H - The sparsely scattered corals of Crocodile Avenue often hide the danger of tropical scorpionfish, Scorpaenopsis barbata.

I - The Bartels mandarin fish, Synchiropus bartelsi, *a member of the* Callionymidae *family, barely reaches four centimeters in length and is difficult to spot.*

A

discoveries. In the first case, the diver will soon notice single specimens or pairs of prickly sea horses, *Hippocampus hystryx*, among the leaves of the algae; small, perfectly camouflaged frogfish; brightly colored newborn cuttlefish only a few centimeters long; rare pipefish, *Sygnathoides biaculeatus*, *Trachyrhamphus longirostris* and *Corythoichtys schultzi*; snake eels from the genus *Myrichtys* with only their heads poking out of the sand; poisonous catfish,

A - A truly unusual encounter: this frogfish, unlike others of its kind, has chosen the muddy substratum of Crocodile Avenue as its habitat.

B - The colors of this tiny harlequin ghost pipefish, Solenostomus paradoxus, *are accentuated by the characteristic white of the young of the species.*

C

B

D

Plotosus lineatus, which cross the sandy stretch in large spherical schools; and individual specimens of *Pterois volitans* turkeyfish, a little incongruous so far from the corals they usually frequent.
A careful examination of the large wooden stumps and branches underwater, will reveal a complex, fascinating universe full of tiny, rare species: adult and young ghost pipefish, *Solenostomus paradoxus*

C - This lionfish, Dendrochirus brachypterus, *rather rare everywhere, can easily be observed among the submerged branches at Crocodile Avenue.*

D - Among the submerged fronds, small members of the Monacanthidae *family,* Acreichthys tomentosum, *can be seen, perfectly camouflaged by plant detritus.*

E

(of different colors), blennies, gobies, incredibly mimetic members of the *Monocanthidae* family, small, multi-hued scorpionfish from the species *Dendrochirus brachypterus*, devil scorpionfish, *Inimicus didactylus*, and stonefish, *Synanceia verrucosa*, hidden in the muddy substratum, flounder, and morays from the genus *Siderea*.
A 90-minute dive in three or four meters of water at Crocodile Avenue will probably cover more rare species than seen in a

E - The devil scorpionfish, Scorpaenopsis diabolus, *is one of the most mimetic inhabitants of the reef, and has one of the most frightening appearances.*

F - A tiny Dendrochirus brachypterus *in a threatening pose menacingly unfolds its pectoral fins in an attempt to frighten the photographer.*

F

I

G

H

lifetime of dives elsewhere. It is also fascinating and extremely easy to do a night dive at this site. Divers are likely to be approached by squadrons of squid, *Sepioteuthis lessoniana*, attracted by their torchlight.

G - Several Manila pufferfish, Arothron manilensis, *can often be seen resting on the sandy seabeds of Crocodile Avenue.*

H - A cuttlefish only a few months old is camouflaged against the plants that grow on the seabed.

I - Two clownfish swim near their anemone of preference, Heteractis aurora.

FROGGY LAIR

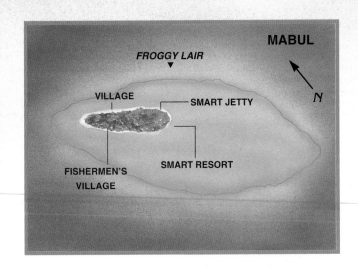

MABUL

FROGGY LAIR ▼

VILLAGE

SMART JETTY

FISHERMEN'S
VILLAGE

SMART RESORT

N

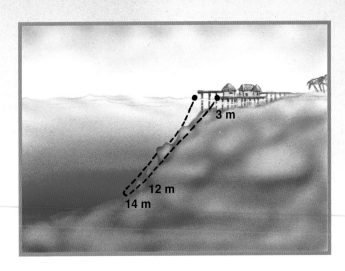

3 m

12 m

14 m

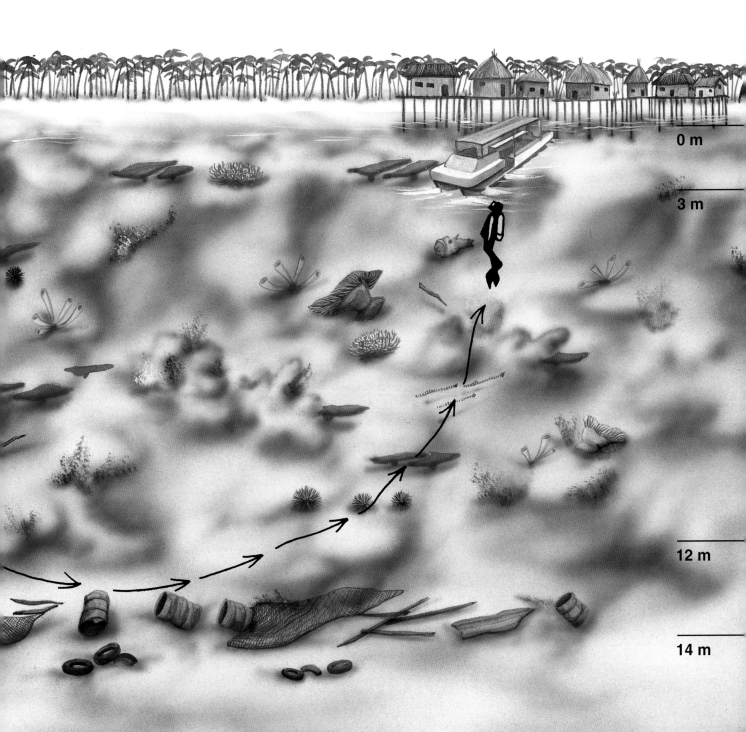

0 m

3 m

12 m

14 m

A

ike Crocodile Avenue, the adjacent Froggy Lair is a diving area which initially seems quite uninviting. Divers enter the water at the tip of the long wooden wharf utilized by the residents of Sipadan-Mabul Resort at low tide, and resurface about a hundred meters away at the foot of the outermost pilework dwellings of Water Village, the other resort on Pulau Mabul. The dive takes place along the straight stretch that joins these two points, at depths that vary from two to 10 meters, along a heavily modified reef that rises with difficulty from a sandy, muddy and detrital seabed. Visibility is in general less than mediocre, the

B

D

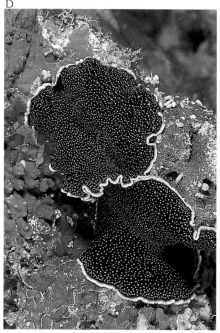

C

A - The jewelbox sea urchin, Tripneustes gratilla, *is one of the most elegant echinoderms on the coral reef.*

B - Because of its daytime habits and liveliness, the peacock mantis shrimp, Odontodactylus scyllaris, *with its extraordinary colors, can often be seen roaming in search of prey.*

C - This photo shows the extraordinary mimetic skills of the crocodile fish, Cymbacephalus beauforti, *characteristic of detrital and sandy seabeds.*

D - Flatworms that belong to the Platyhelminthes *family often have extraordinarily decorative colors.*

quantity of suspended particles is quite high (especially in the afternoon, during the tide) and the corals are rare and stunted. These coral formations are suffocated by the mud deposited on them, or even covered with fragments of old, coarse fishing nets, old tires, rotting branches and tangled nylon nets. Here and there the slope is interrupted by little landslides of detrital material and dead coral. At about 10 meters deep the true muddy seabed begins, characteristic of the dives at Crocodile Avenue further on.

However, any initial discomfort will soon transform into wonder when this classic "muck dive" begins to reveal its tiny, fascinating treasures.

At the base of the coral formations divers will probably see perfectly camouflaged frogfish (which give their name to the area) lying in wait on the candelabra sponges; crocodile fish, *Cymbacephalus beauforti* and *Thysanophrys otaitensis,* of every age and size (the immature specimens are especially interesting: only a little longer than a pencil, they are perfectly camouflaged by twigs or dead leaves and are quite different from the adults of the species, which are also mimetic but richly decorated with brown and turquoise hues); diurnal and nocturnal cowries; various species

E

F

G

E - Disturbed by the presence of the photographer, a dangerous devil scorpionfish, Scorpaenopsis diabolus, *moves awkwardly on the sand, using the free rays of its pectoral fins as toes.*

F - This close-up shows a scorpionfish, Scorpaenopsis macrochir, *less than 10 centimeters long and quite similar to its relative* diabolus, *the devil scorpionfish.*

G - Like a jewel lost in the sand, the nudibranch Phyllidia ocellata *is one of the most common nudibranchs on the seabeds of Mabul and Kapalai.*

A

of nudibranchs in all sizes; den gobies (don't miss the splendid *Sygnigobius biocellatus*, whose intimidating profile and movements mimic the form of a crab); seawhip corals (the timid and semi-transparent *Bryaninops loki* always ready to move to the other side of the whip if a diver comes too close); members of the *Opisthognathidae* family (especially *Opisthognathus aurifrons*, which is immediately recognizable by its bright gold "eyebrows" that decorate its velvety brown snout, as it peeps out of its vertical tunnel dug into the substratum); cleaner shrimp from the genus *Periclemenes*, which live as guests in the large

B

C

D

A - Flatworms in the Platyhelminthe *family are some of the most colorful and spectacular creatures on the coral reef. Pictured is the splendid* Pseudoceros affinis.

B - The snout of a variegated lizardfish, Synodus variegatus, *lying in wait, pokes out motionlessly from the detrital substratum of Froggy Lair.*

C - Adult harlequin ghost pipefish, Solenostromus paradoxus, *sport bright colors but are nevertheless highly mimetic.*

D - Among the most interesting species at Froggy Lair is the Sygnigobius biocellatus *goby, which fools predators into mistaking it for a crab by its combination of colors and jumping movements.*

anemones; rare and fascinating ghost pipefish (both *Solenostomus cyanopterus* and the even stranger *Solenostomus paradoxus*); and numerous species of the *Syngnathidae* family, some of the most beautiful of which are the ringed pipefish, *Doryrhamphus dactyliophorus*. As in all muck dives, divers must take care with their position, as uncontrolled movements may raise clouds of fine suspended particles that would reduce visibility almost to zero. Another reason to concentrate on buoyancy control is the fact that hidden in the sand and nearly invisible are numerous devil scorpionfish, *Inimicus didactylus,*

E

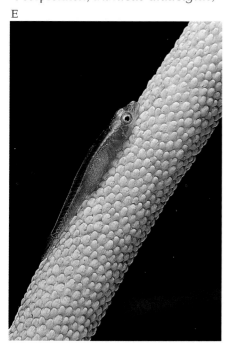

false stonefish, *Scorpaenopsis diabolus,* and the stonefish *Synanceia verrucosa,* not to mention hundreds of sea urchins, *Diaderna setosum,* wreathing the corals with their long, extremely fragile spines. They are fascinating, but can cause very serious and painful wounds.

F

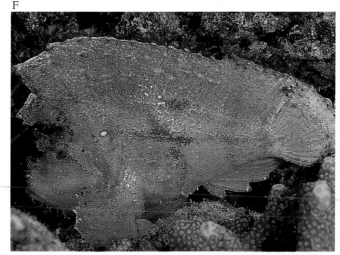

G

H

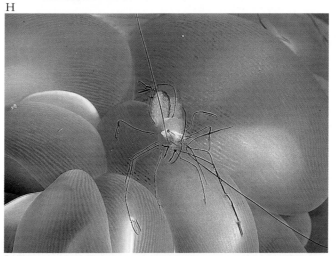

I

E - *Rare at shallow depths, sea whips from the genus Juncella host numerous symbiotic gobies,* Bryaninops ampulus.

F - *One of the characteristics of the leaf scorpionfish,* Taenianotus triacanthus, *is the capacity to shed its external layer of skin in a single molting, like snakes.*

G - *This close-up shows the snout of a young crocodile fish,* Cymbacephalus beauforti, *with its characteristic dark color. Note the eye protected by the mobile, palpebral fringes.*

H - *It is not uncommon to find beautiful transparent shrimp from the genus* Periclemenes *among the tentacles of bubble corals,* Pterogyra flexuosa.

I - *This pair of pipefish,* Corythoichthys amplexus, *was surprised during their courting ritual. At Froggy Lair it is common to see various species of pipefish during a single dive.*

LAYANG LAYANG

WRASSE STRIP ▼

CRACK REEF ▼

GORGONIAN FOREST ▼

THE VALLEY ▼

SHARK'S CAVE ▼

" D" WALL ▼

Inland Lagoon

LAYANG LAYANG ISLAND RESORT

Reef

THE TUNNEL ▼

WRECK POINT ▼

N

Occupying a total surface area of 14 square kilometres, the atoll of Layang Layang is situated in the South China Sea about 300 kilometers off the coast of Borneo, in the heart of the Indo-Pacific area, which has the richest wildlife and greatest marine biodiversity in the world. Geographically, it belongs to the disputed Spratley Archipelago, but politically it is part of Malaysia. Indeed, the Malaysian government has deliberately transformed a tiny

virtually unprecedented for divers. Indeed, the Layang Layang reef offers all the advantages of a site accessible only by live-aboard boat (absolute isolation, virgin seabeds, large specimens of pelagic species and very few visitors) without the problems related to life on board. The surrounding seabeds offer at least a dozen excellent diving sites, characterized by shallow depths with extraordinary coral gardens teeming with reef microfauna, full of steep drop-offs into the abyss

inexpert divers.

The coral gardens (especially in the diving areas known as Crack Reef, Wrasse Strip and Navigator's Lane) boast colonies of *Acropora*, *Xenia*, *Montipora*, *Turbinaria*, *Porites* and *Sarcophyton* of astounding richness and incredible complexity, among which intact and fragile branches swim hundreds of different species of fish, crustaceans and mollusks, some common, others less so, and yet others extremely rare or even still unclassified. Here are multi-

A

B

portion of the emerging coral reef into a small artificial island to affirm its political and military presence here.
The unusual origins of the area - the construction of a Malaysian naval base was followed by the development of a modern tourist resort - have made it a destination

and the almost constant presence of open sea species. The coral reef that encircles the atoll's immense lagoon has remained untouched for thousands of years, has never been fished, has experienced no pollution of any kind, and has never suffered the devastating kicks of hordes of enthusiastic but

hued clouds of butterflyfish from the genus *Chaetodon*, triggerfish, *Odonus niger*, flanked by elegant angelfish, *Pomacanthus imperator* and *xanthometopon*. numerous species of garishly hued parrotfish from the genus *Scarus*, large anemones, *Heteractis magnifica*, with symbiotic clownfish from the genus *Amphiprion*, porcelain crabs from the genus *Neopetrolisthes* and shrimp from the genus *Periclemenes*.

The atoll of Layang Layang arises like a gigantic tower isolated by waters more than 2,000 meters deep, and its well-known distance from the continental shelf makes it possible to dive in water which is generally crystal clear, with horizontal visibility that exceeds 50 meters, all quite unusual in this part of the world.

Every wall of the atoll (especially in Gorgonian Forest, The Point and Dogtooth Lair) provides enormous thrills and stupefying encounters: giant mantas, *Manta birostris*, schools of enormous dogtooth tunas, *Gymnosarda unicolor*, eagle rays, *Aetobatus narinari*, grey reef sharks, *Carcharhinus amblyrhynchos*, squadrons of *Sphyraena barracuda*, *qenie* and *flavicauda* barracudas, formations of batfish from the genus *Platax*, large sea urchins from the genus *Seriola*, the rare fox sharks, *Alopias vulpinus*, gigantic schools of scalloped hammerhead sharks, *Sphyrna lewini*, and sometimes even an occasional whale shark, *Rinchodon typus*, or a solitary oceanic whitetip shark, *Carcharhinus longimanus*.

And there's more. Some diving areas on the wall (in particular "D" Wall, Crack Reef and Shark's Cave) have balconies and terraces that interrupt the drop-off at a depth of about 30 meters, providing an ideal setting for encounters with rare nudibranchs, den gobies with symbiotic crayfish, stingrays, *Taeniura melanospilos*, and blue-spotted ribbontail stingrays, *Taeniura lymma*, leopard sharks, *Stegostoma fasciatum*, and whitetip reef sharks, *Triaenodon obesus*. All this in a fascinating panorama dominated by enormous barrel sponges, *Xestospongia testudinaria*, gigantic yellow and orange gorgonians wreathed by crinoids in a thousand colors and formidable colonies of red seawhip corals from the genus *Eunicella*.

C

D

E

A - This photo taken from an airplane shows the atoll of Layang Layang and its broad reef.

B - The vertical drop-offs of Layang Layang are characterized by gigantic fans of gorgonians and excellent visibility.

C - The top reef of the atoll has remained intact due to its centuries of isolation. Pictured is a lovely group of orange anthias and a clown triggerfish, Balistoides conspicullum, swimming near the coral wall.

D - Underwater photography fans will find numerous immobile subjects of great interest, such as this crinoid, in the waters of Layang Layang.

E - By looking out to the endless sea, you may observe spectacular groups of pelagic fauna, such as sharks, tunas and silvery bigeye trevallies, Caranx sexfasciatus, like those shown in the photo.

To complete the picture, even the less-frequented sites characterized by coral formations crumbled by the surf (such as in The Valley) or by deep fissures in the walls (such as The Tunnel, ideal for interesting night explorations) can offer unexpected excitement.

All the day dives take place from boats in areas which are only a few minutes from the diving center's small pier. The set schedules must be followed scrupulously, with groups as homogenous as possible, and a detailed briefing always precedes each dive.

The divemaster acts as an observer only, and divers must use the buddy system. As might be imagined, the use of a wrist computer is highly recommended (maximum permitted depth is 40 meters, but be careful - in water so clear it is easy to accumulate excessive decompression times), and the consumption of alcohol during the day is discouraged.

GORGONIAN FOREST

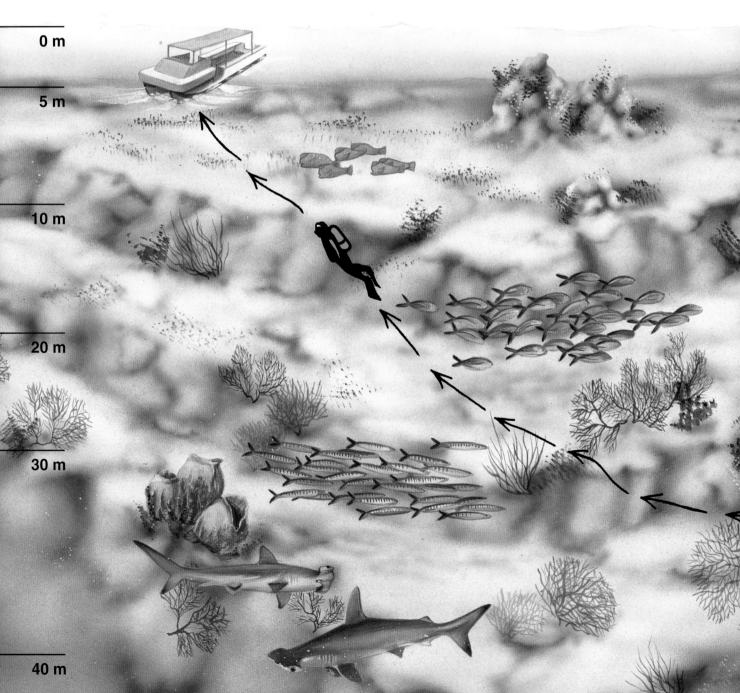

0 m

5 m

10 m

20 m

30 m

40 m

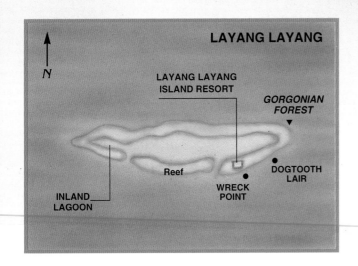

LAYANG LAYANG

N

LAYANG LAYANG
ISLAND RESORT

*GORGONIAN
FOREST*

Reef

INLAND
LAGOON

WRECK
POINT

DOGTOOTH
LAIR

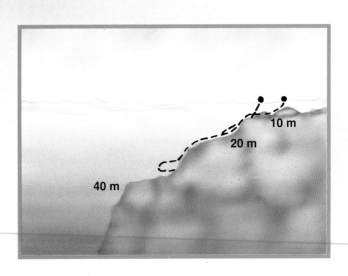

10 m

20 m

40 m

A - Along the drop-off of Gorgonian Forest it is common to see large schools of barracuda, Sphyraena putnamiae *and* Sphyraena jello *(shown in the photo).*

B - As its name denotes, the forest of gorgonians located at a depth of between 30 and 60 meters is characteristic of the site.

Along with the exploration of the adjacent sites, Wreck's Point and Dogtooth Lair, probably the most beautiful dive at Layang Layang, and one of the most spectacular and enthralling in this part of the world, is along the seabeds of Gorgonian Forest. The site is characterized by the nearly constant presence of a strong current running parallel to the wall, creating an extraordinary horizontal visibility which often exceeds 50 meters.

A

B

C

D

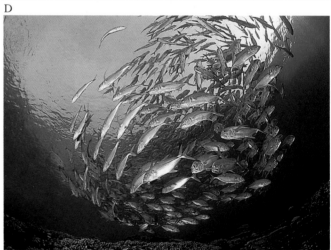

Interesting encounters occur along the wall, and at medium and deeper depths near the drop-off and in open water on leaving the wall, which is not vertical, but more like a steep slope. The dive begins on a shallow seabed about five to 10 meters deep, just a few fin strokes away from the actual drop-off, where it plunges steeply. Once divers reach their desired depth, they should move first horizontally and then make a gradual ascent, keeping the wall to

C - Particularly spectacular and luxuriant, the colonies of whip gorgonians from the genus Elisella *at Gorgonian Forest offer photographers quite lovely shots.*

D - As at Sipadan, the drop-offs of Layang Layang are home to gigantic vortices of hundreds of bigeye trevallies, Caranx sexfasciatus, *here set off by the particular luminosity of the water.*

E - Between March and April at Gorgonian Forest it is common to see large concentrations of barracuda, Sphyraena putnamiae.

F - One of the most common sharks along the drop-offs of Layang Layang is the timid whitetip reef shark, Triaenodon obesus, *a little over 1.5 meters in length.*

their right with the current in their favor. The seabed, initially characterized by a somewhat rough coral shallows full of bommie and coral towers, plunges in a steep slope full of terraces, balconies, small recesses and caves. The area gets its name from an astounding forest of gorgonians, many of which are huge and in perfect condition, with gigantic orange fans that stretch out into the current throughout the dive, at depths varying from 30-50 meters. Alternating with superb colonies of scarlet whip corals in the genera *Eunicella* and *Melithaea* and enormous barrel sponges in the genus *Xestospongia*, the gorgonians form a highly unusual forest, giving underwater photographers extraordinary views and shots from below, especially in the morning. The incredible transparency of the water adds to the effect. Indeed, it is the exceptional visibility that, along with the strong current, permits the exciting encounters that are typical of Gorgonian Forest. At shallow and medium depths, on or near the

G

H

terrace, there are schools of surgeonfish, *Naso* and *Acanthurus*, phalanxes of great barracuda, *Sphyraena barracuda*, and blackstripe barracuda, *Sphyraena putnamiae*, schools of batfish, *Platax orbicularis*, small groups and single specimens of massive bumphead parrotfish, *Bolbometopon muricatum*, and a surprising myriad of reef species, especially numerous varieties of butterflyfish from the genera *Chaetodon* and *Heniochus*, and many species of tropical groupers.

E

F

G - While it generally remains in deep waters, the silvertip shark, Carcharhinus albimarginatus, *may occasionally make spectacular appearances at shallower depths.*

H - The menacing profile of a scalloped hammerhead shark, Sphyrna lewini, *nearly three meters long, stands out against the surface of the South China Sea.*

In the open water, not far from the wall and at medium depth, hover immense spherical schools of bigeye trevallies, *Caranx sexfasciatus*, while compact formations of dogtooth tuna, *Gymnosarda unicolor*, which are larger here and travel in bigger schools than almost anywhere else, glide by.

At greater depths, which are absolutely not recommended for sport dives, there are many grey reef sharks, *Carcharhinus amblyrhynchos* (sometimes in groups of up to 30 individuals),

A - The relatively common tomato anemonefish, Amphiprion frenatus, *is associated exclusively with the anemone* Entacmaea quadricolor.

A

B

C

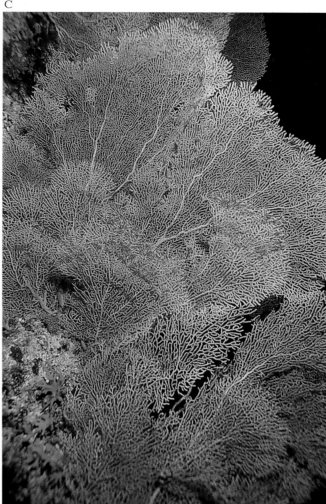

and isolated examples of rare fox sharks, *Alopias vulpinus* or *superciliosus*.

If the diver turns his attention from the blue depths to the coral slope, he is likely to see numerous creatures hidden in the recesses of the wall, including large stingrays, *Taeniura melanospylos*, and blue-spotted ribbontail stingrays, *Taeniura lymma*, and even an enormous sleeping nurse shark, *Nebrius ferrugineus*.

But it is the open water that provides the most excitement at Gorgonian Forest. At the right time of year, between April and May, divers are likely to encounter large schools of scalloped hammerhead sharks, *Sphyrna lewini*, which gather here to perform their mating rituals. Or they may see the courting rites of bigeye trevallies, *Caranx sexfasciatus*, and gigantic bumphead parrotfish, *Bolbometopon muricatum*, or unexpectedly witness a band of dogtooth tuna engage in an attack on a school of bigeye trevallies, distracted by the pangs of love.

B - The pink clownfish, Amphiprion perideraion, *lives with various species of anemones, including the spectacular* Heteractis magnifica.

C - The gigantic gorgonians of Gorgonian Forest have few equals in the world, and the largest colonies exceed 2.5 meters in diameter.

D

inducing them to go too deep or reach excessively lengthy decompression times. Unforgettable dives can be experienced at Gorgonian Forest at reasonable depths, within 30 meters, without going too far from the wall. Indeed, there is a risk that divers may lose sight of the wall and find themselves out in the open sea at the mercy of the current, which changes direction suddenly in front of Dogtooth Lair, disorienting even the most seasoned divers when they have no visual point of reference.

E - During the spring the top reef of Layang Layang is often frequented by large schools of gigantic parrotfish, Bolbometopon muricatum, awaiting the mating season.

F - Batfish, Platax teira, live in small groups. Due to their extraordinary elegance, they are particularly appreciated by underwater photographers.

G - Every exploration of the walls of Layang Layang reveals a myriad of interesting subjects for photographers and naturalists. Pictured is a lovely bush of whip coral in an extraordinary shade of red.

H - The photographer's lens has captured an enormous gorgonian fan, the pride and glory of the vertiginous drop-off at Gorgonian Forest.

E

G

F

H

D - The leopard shark, Stegostoma fasciatum, is a harmless and frequent resident of the deeper sandy terraces of Gorgonian Forest.

Also during this period one or more whale sharks, *Rinchodon typus,* may make a punctual but fleeting visit in the open waters near Gorgonian Forest, providing a brief but unforgettable spectacle for divers who are making their mandatory safety stop in the open water away from the wall.
An important comment: the extraordinary visibility that characterizes this site and the exciting variety of encounters may deceive less cautious divers,

WRECK POINT

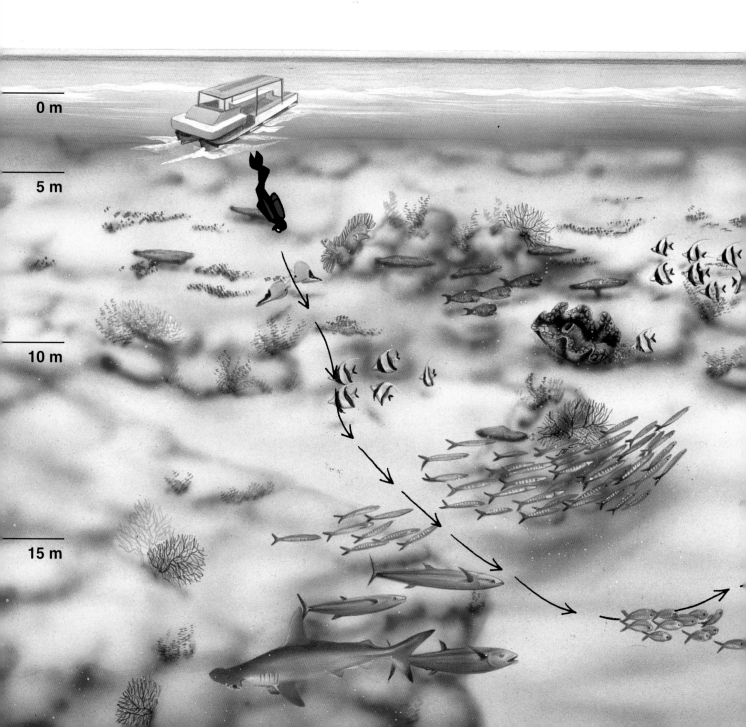

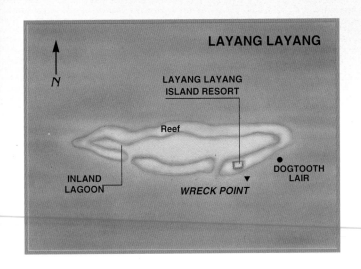

LAYANG LAYANG

N

LAYANG LAYANG
ISLAND RESORT

Reef

INLAND
LAGOON

DOGTOOTH
LAIR

WRECK POINT

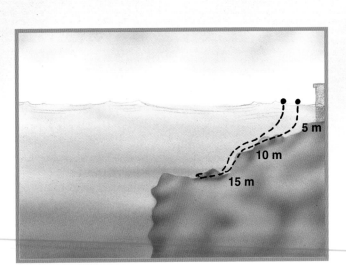

5 m

10 m

15 m

Continuing on from Dogtooth Lair, which is really an integral part of Gorgonian Forest, the site of Wreck Point takes its name from the wreck of an old freighter, no trace of which remains today except for a few pieces of scrap iron in the sand. Thus, instead of an exploration of submerged vessels, this site offers a pleasant, relaxing, shallow-to-medium depth tour of an elegant coral garden directly opposite the reinforced concrete containment wall that surrounds the emerging portion of the Layang Layang atoll.

Due to its position, Wreck Point is primarily visited as the conclusion

C

A - *The gigantic specimens of* Tridacna maxima *which have developed in the waters of Wreck Point are an exceptional point of interest for divers. These gastropods have become rare throughout the Indo-Pacific due to overfishing.*

B - *At a relatively shallow depth are many enormous specimens of barrel sponges,* Xestospongia testudinaria.

C - *The reef of Layang Layang is most luxuriant near the surface. The photograph shows several extraordinary bushes of gorgonians which have achieved remarkable dimensions.*

D - *A typical resident of the coral is the elegant, multicolored bistred hawkfish,* Paracirrhites arcatus, *an able predator less than 15 centimeters long.*

A

D

B

of the much more difficult dives at Gorgonian Forest and Dogtooth Lair, when its shallow seabed is used for the required safety stop, perhaps with a last glance at the now distant depths where only a few minutes ago one swam in the company of grey reef sharks and hammerheads.

This is a mistake, however, because this site alone provides excellent dives. In the deepest areas, where the slope suddenly becomes steep, transforming into a precipitous cliff, divers are likely to encounter schools of dogtooth tuna, *Gymnosarda unicolor*, as they ride on the current, with an immense spherical school of several hundred bigeye trevallies

which move along the wall during the day, a few phalanxes of barracuda coming in from the blue depths, and perhaps even a rare nurse shark, *Nebrius ferrugineus*, or a solitary hammerhead rising up from below. At medium to shallow depths, on the reef summit, it is difficult not to be enchanted by the fragile gardens of lettuce coral, *Pavona cactus*, which extend for dozens of square meters, or the immense "mushrooms" formed by colonies of 3,000-year-old *Porites*, or the astounding variety of species which share the complex habitat of the coral reef. Some of the most easily

E - This clownfish, Amphiprion frenatus, lives symbiotically with its chosen anemone, Entacmaea quadricolor, recognizable by the characteristically swollen tips of its tentacles.

F - The passage of a group of batfish, Platax teira, provides a scene of rare grace and elegance.

G - The beautiful peacock flounder, Bothus mancus, may occasionally be observed in the shallower portions of the reef, often just a few centimeters from the surface.

H - Schools of barracuda, Sphyraena putnamiae and Sphyraena jello, are easy to spot at Wreck Point.

I - This spectacular shot is of the characteristic spherical schools of bigeye trevallies, Caranx sexfasciatus, which can be observed during April and May near Wreck Point and Gorgonian Forest.

observable creatures at a shallow depth include the numerous species of parrotfish from the genus *Scarus*, butterflyfish such as those in the genus *Chaetodon*, and clown anemonefish from the *Amphiprion* genus, symbiotic with sea anemones.

Rare elsewhere, but extremely common here, are groups of refined Moorish idols, *Zanclus cornutus*, schools of batfish, *Platax orbicularis* and *Platax teira*, and the dense schools of *Sphyraena flavicauda*, or ocean pike. Both at Wreck Point and in the immediate vicinity, it is possible to admire several enormous giant clams, *Tridacna maxima*, bivalves of impressive

size (a diver and all his equipment can fit comfortably in some of them) which have unfortunately become extremely rare throughout the entire Indo-Pacific due to overfishing.

Given the marine orography - an emerging reef with a sandy bottom, characterized by large coral bommies full of crevices and cavities with wide stretches of extensively branched *Acropora* corals - it is difficult to suggest one Wreck Point itinerary over another. Indeed, its coral structure, in pleasant disarray at a shallow depth, makes it ideal for highly satisfying night dives as well.

THE TUNNEL

INDIA

THE PHILIPPINES

LAYANG
LAYANG

PACIFIC
OCEAN

MALAYSIA

BORNEO

PAPUA
NEW GUINEA

INDONESIA

INDIAN OCEAN

AUSTRALIA

N

0 m

5 m

10 m

15 m

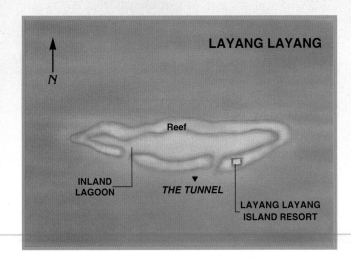

LAYANG LAYANG

N

Reef

INLAND
LAGOON

THE TUNNEL

LAYANG LAYANG
ISLAND RESORT

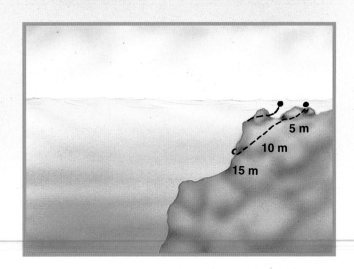

5 m

10 m

15 m

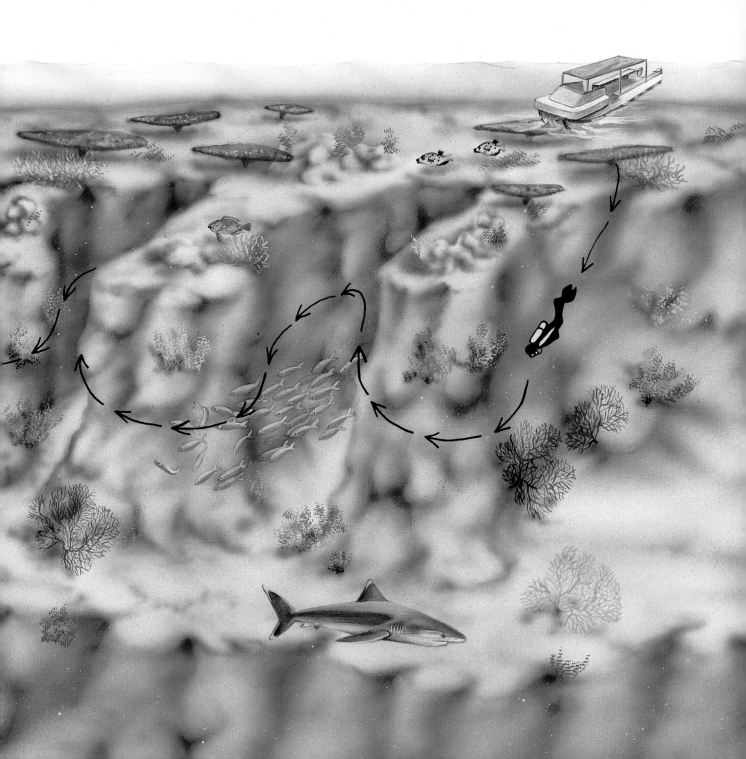

U nderstandably but unjustly overshadowed by the numerous other diving areas of Layang Layang which certainly offer more spectacular encounters, a dive at The Tunnel can nevertheless reveal many interesting sights and unusual camera shots.

Given its quite unique conformation and sheltered position, it offers few possibilities for encounters with large pelagic species, and thus permits photographers to concentrate on the small creatures present here in great numbers (mollusks, small crustaceans and crinoids), which elsewhere would inevitably be ignored. Another specimen which should not be overlooked is an enormous, splendid fan of *Dendrophyllia* green coral, stiffly

A

B

C

D

E

A - The drop-off at The Tunnel is adorned with an elegant colony of very large Dendrophyllia, an excellent subject for underwater photographers during the day.

B - This view of the wall reveals the extraordinary variety of colors and the biological complexity of the reef of Layang Layang.

C - In the shadow of the drop-off it is not uncommon to see longfin bannerfish, Heniochus acuminatus, *which are either solitary or travel in pairs.*

D - A night-time exploration of the crevices at The Tunnel reveals extraordinary fauna, in particular large hermit crabs from the genus Dardanus.

E - Usually hidden during the day, the spotted lionfish, Pterois antennata, *takes advantage of the dark to go hunting.*

and delicately extended into the blue depths: be careful not to damage its elegant branches. The wall along which the dive takes place is most interesting in the first 10 meters of depth, where the coral opens into a series of deep vertical cracks which a diver can easily enter, with chimneys that vary in size until the last one transforms into a true canyon.

It goes without saying that such rough terrain over only a few dozen square meters, easily explorable during a single dive, offers an infinite number of shelters and microenvironments which are ideal for small, highly specialized species.

It is not worth the effort to descend too deep, because below 15 meters the cracks in the wall close and the wall, temporarily interrupted by a sand and coral detritus terrace,

*F - This rare
and spectacular
starfish seems
to be posing for
the photographer.*

*G - A graceful
crinoid from the
genus Comanthina
takes advantage
of dusk to capture
plankton.*

*H - Tiny and
semitransparent,
this goby from the
genus Eviota has
marked off its
territory on a patch
of Diploastrea
heliopora coral.*

*I - This gigantic
specimen of a
blackspotted
pufferfish, Arothron
stellatus, is resting
in the shade of a
coral formation.*

plunges straight into the abyss. It is better to explore the shallow environments thoroughly, by visiting The Tunnel as the third dive of the day or, better yet, as a night dive. If the dive takes place just after twilight it is possible to linger in just a few square meters of space, observing by flashlight all the twilight and nocturnal creatures that have finally abandoned the crevices in which they shelter during daylight hours.

This is the best time to admire the multi-hued crinoids from the genera *Oxycomanthus*, *Comaster* and *Comanthina* that wreathe the tops of the gorgonians and the coral fans, their long pinnules reaching out into the current to capture the plankton on which these ancient animals feed.

G

H

I

F

Among the moving "arms" are usually tiny crustaceans - crayfish and their fellow squat lobster - which perfectly mimic the colors of their host.

They are usually invisible during the day, when the crinoids close up and withdraw into the fissures of the reef. Also present may be the gorgonian starfish, always ready to withdraw into itself as soon as it is disturbed by the light of the torches, or a myriad

of crayfish (especially from the genus *Stenopus*), hermit crabs, sea urchins, crabs and starfish scouting among the corals.

It is easy to spot sleeping fish among the coral branches, especially pufferfish from the genus *Arothron*, parrotfish from the genus *Scarus* and fusiliers from the genus *Caesio*, or predators lying silently in wait, such as *Pterois volitans* and *radiata* turkeyfish.

"D" WALL

INDIA

THE PHILIPPINES

PACIFIC OCEAN

LAYANG
LAYANG

MALAYSIA

N

BORNEO

PAPUA
NEW GUINEA

INDONESIA

INDIAN OCEAN

AUSTRALIA

0 m

5 m

10 m

20 m

40 m

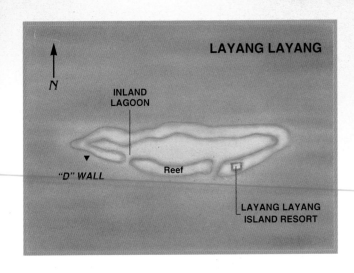

LAYANG LAYANG

N

INLAND
LAGOON

"D" WALL

Reef

LAYANG LAYANG
ISLAND RESORT

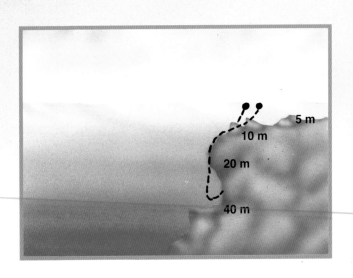

5 m

10 m

20 m

40 m

No-one knows how this wall earned its name, but it is one of the very few truly vertical walls on the Layang Layang atoll. Situated along a steep drop-off that plunges for over 2,000 meters into the abyss of the South China Sea, its fascination is increased by the extraordinary transparency of the water. The vertical structure is interrupted only by a wide ledge at a depth of about 40 meters. Here, after a quick descent straight down, is a sandy balcony about 30 meters long and five or six meters wide. Shaded by a vault jutting out from the wall, it protrudes like a magical balcony toward the cobalt blue of the open sea. This site is ideal for a pause that should be exploited to the maximum, while remaining within safety limits. The shelf is richly encrusted with a formidable concentration of benthonic organisms, especially enormous barrel sponges from the genus *Xestospongia*, and vigorous fans of gorgonians, among which lie several large turkeyfish, *Pterois volitans*. Further down, the depths are illuminated by the fluorescent violet flashes of the elegant *Pseudanthias pleurotaenia*, large tropical anthias which, unlike their more common cousins the *tuka*, or purple anthias, prefer deep water. The majestic projecting vault is wreathed by enormous gorgonians, some of which are

C

A

D

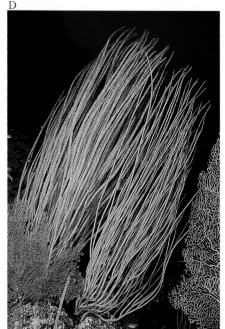

B

amazingly large, and are in their turn adorned with plumes of multicolored crinoids, vigorous alcyonarians from the genus *Dendronephthya*, with their delicate pastel hues, an immense bush of black coral from the genus *Antipatharia*, and other gigantic barrel sponges.

It is unfortunate that at this depth divers have only a limited amount of time available, because the balcony offers numerous extraordinary shots for macro-photography fans.

The depth and shade make it a true hothouse for rare nudibranchs, small crustaceans alongside sea anemones and crinoids, various species of den gobies and tiny

A - The vertical drop-off at "D" Wall is adorned by numerous large specimens of sponges, some of which are big enough for a diver to climb into.

B - It is not uncommon to see giant mantas, Manta birostris, along the wall, especially in April and May.

C - Along the sides of "D" wall are numerous gorgonians, with fans which are often over two meters long.

D - A dense colony of whip gorgonians, Elisella andamanensis, illuminates the deeper seabeds.

E - On the edge of the sandy terraces of "D" Wall are several enormous sea anemones, Heteractis magnifica, inhabited by a large number of clownfish.

Bryaninops loki gobies which have made their homes in the fronds and whips of the *Juncella* black corals. "D" Wall certainly deserves to be visited more than once. In addition to the small wonders that inhabit it, it is also the best site in the entire Layang Layang atoll for spotting large specimens of leopard sharks, *Stegostoma fasciatum*, which often rest on the sandy floor of the balcony, sometimes in the company of smaller and more timid whitetip reef sharks, *Triaenodon obesus*. If the season is right, it is also not uncommon to see large schools of scalloped hammerhead sharks, *Sphyrna lewini*, passing close by as they emerge from the open

F

E

G

H

sea, while at greater depths it is common to see grey reef sharks, *Carcharhinus amblyrhynchos* (be careful of younger, smaller individuals: they are very curious and potentially more aggressive than adults). At "D" Wall divers are also likely to see a young manta ray, *Manta birostris*, which seems to have become sedentary, with a marked preference for this area. The dive concludes with a gradual diagonal ascent, keeping the wall to the divers' right until they reach the luxuriant coral gardens that crown the top of the reef, where the necessary safety stop can be made.

F - On the edge of the sandy terraces of "D" Wall it is easy to approach large leopard sharks, Stegostoma fasciatum. *Despite their meek nature, you should always avoid touching these sharks or annoying them. If disturbed, they can inflict painful bites.*

G - The brightly colored, gregarious peach anthias (the specimen pictured is a male) lives in large schools on the surface areas of the reef of D Wall.

H - A timid ray seeks refuge under the sandy layer that covers the seabed.

THE VALLEY

INDIA

THE PHILIPPINES

PACIFIC OCEAN

*LAYANG
LAYANG*

MALAYSIA

N

BORNEO

PAPUA
NEW GUINEA

INDIAN OCEAN

INDONESIA

AUSTRALIA

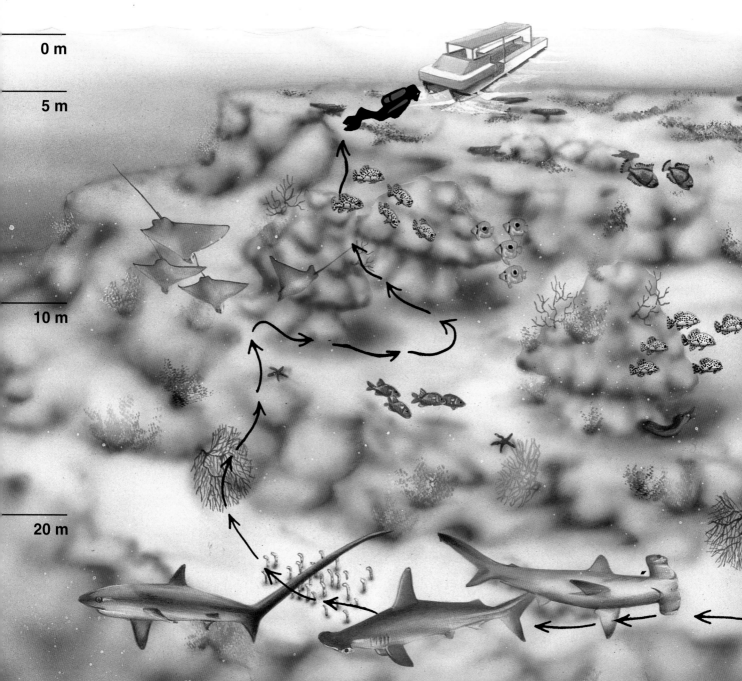

0 m

5 m

10 m

20 m

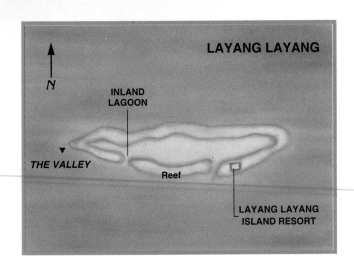

LAYANG LAYANG

N

INLAND
LAGOON

THE VALLEY

Reef

LAYANG LAYANG
ISLAND RESORT

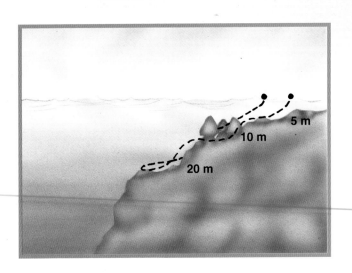

5 m

10 m

20 m

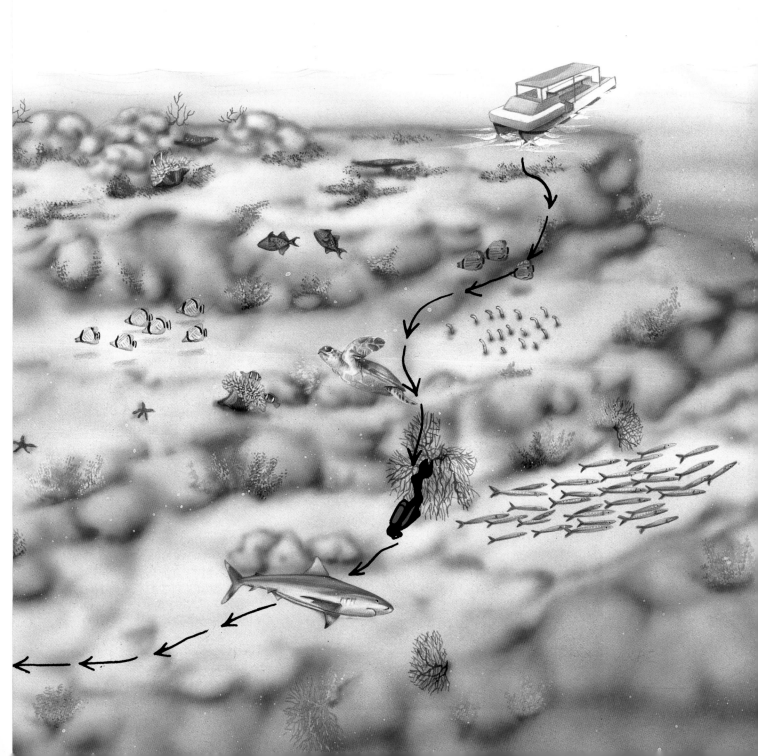

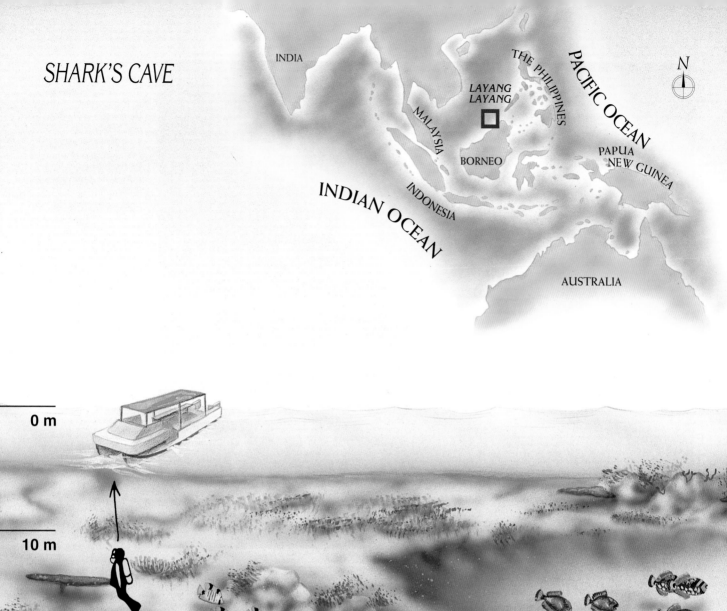

SHARK'S CAVE

INDIA

MALAYSIA

LAYANG LAYANG

THE PHILIPPINES

PACIFIC OCEAN

BORNEO

INDONESIA

INDIAN OCEAN

PAPUA NEW GUINEA

AUSTRALIA

N

0 m

10 m

20 m

30 m

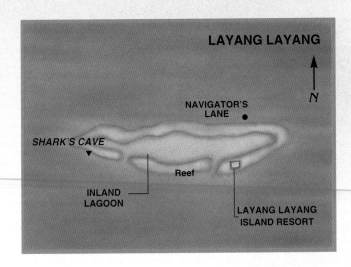

LAYANG LAYANG

NAVIGATOR'S LANE

SHARK'S CAVE

Reef

INLAND LAGOON

LAYANG LAYANG ISLAND RESORT

N

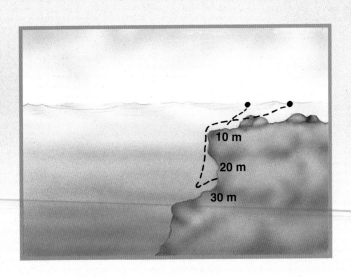

10 m

20 m

30 m

A - The vertical drop-off at Shark's Cave is characterized by a large number of luxuriant, brightly colored sea fan gorgonians.

B - There is no lack of splendid alcyonarians from the genus Dendronephthya in these waters.

C - A diver observes closely a large barrel sponge.

D - This colony of bubble corals, Plerogyra flexuosa, is an unusual green color.

E - This large gorgonian belongs to the genus Melithaea.

F - This close-up of a large whitetip reef shark, Triaenodon obesus, shows its odd teeth.

G - At Shark's Cave encounters with leopard sharks, Stegostoma fasciatum, are frequent.

H - In these waters it is not uncommon to see a majestic giant manta, Manta birostris, heading out toward the open water.

C

A

B

D

E

The area known as Shark's Cave is adjacent to "D" Wall and has more or less the same characteristics: an intact top reef with luxuriant growth and an amazing variety of resident species, a vertiginous vertical drop and a sandy balcony, in this case at a depth of about 30 meters, located on a gentle slope. It is here that divers are likely to encounter large leopard sharks, *Stegostoma fasciatum*, and smaller whitetip reef sharks, *Triaenodon obesus*, which are timid and easy to approach. All around, from the surface to the depths, is the customary, sumptuous panorama typical of

the walls of the Layang Layang atoll: gigantic *Suberogorgia* and *Syphonogorgia* gorgonians that reach out into the depths, dense colonies of *Antipatharia* black corals in the shadow of the jutting vaults, gigantic barrel sponges, *Xestospongia*, and a myriad of *Scleractinia* and other corals and sponges in every size and shape. About halfway through the dive, when divers diagonally ascend along the wall, right after the balcony at a depth of about 25 meters, is a large, wide cavity which can be ventured into for five or six meters. Move very cautiously, however, as the floor is of extremely fine sand, and the bubbles from an air tank will immediately begin to disturb the vault, detaching millions of encrusted particles. Photographers should minimize the emission of air bubbles to avoid rapidly reducing visibility.

The interior offers a superb spectacle, with the vivid blue of the open sea framed by the mouth of the grotto, which in its turn is wreathed by gigantic gorgonians similar to bright orange lace, with feathery colonies of stony corals,as white and airy as clouds of cotton candy. Sometimes groups of whitetip reef sharks, leopard sharks, or much more rarely, sleeping nurse sharks, *Nebrius ferrugineus*, may be encountered in the cavern. Although these sharks are generally harmless to divers, they should not be disturbed. Above all, divers should not place themselves between the animals and the mouth of the cavern so as to block their possible exit.

During this dive, keep an eye on the open sea, as it is not uncommon to see grey reef sharks, *Carcharhinus amblyrhynchos*, giant mantas, *Manta birostris*, eagle rays, *Aetobatus narinari* and, during the mating season, from March to May, schools of scalloped hammerheads, *Sphyrna lewini*, passing by in the depths.

A slow, gradual ascent will bring divers to the splendid top coral reef, where they can pass the rest of the dive at shallow depths, exploring the intact colonies of *Acropora*, *Turbinaria*, *Xenia* and *Porites* which characterize it. This is an opportunity to admire an enormous quantity of species typical of the reef, from the brightly colored emperor angelfish and clown anemonefish to the smaller, timid blennies which, in a riot of color, just barely peep out from their lairs among the corals.

F

G

H

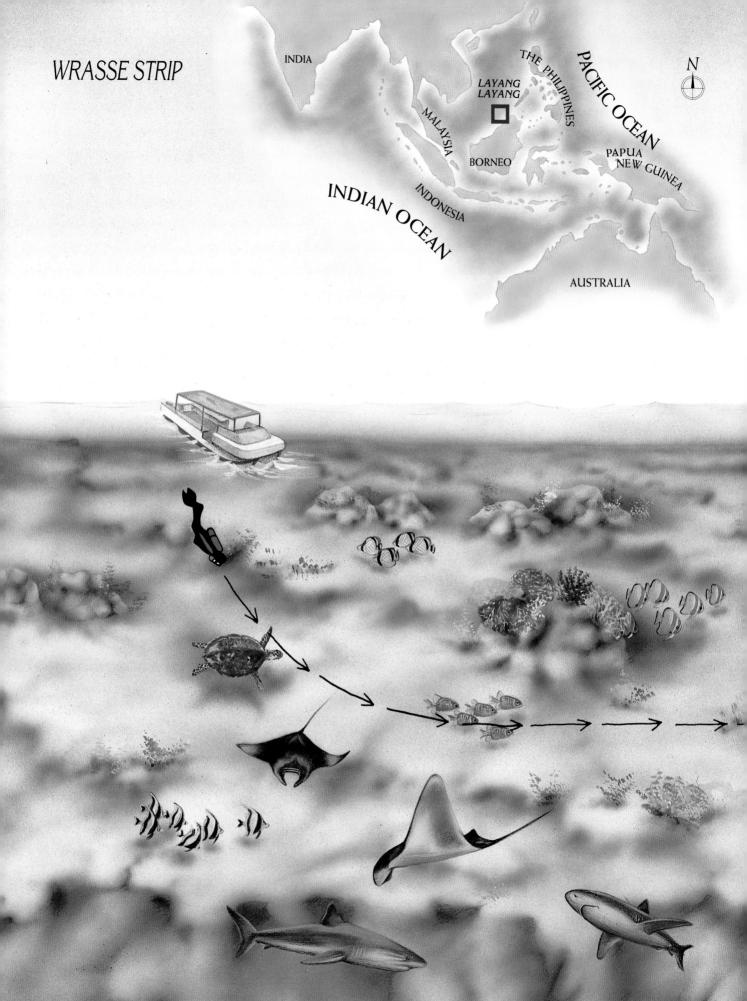

WRASSE STRIP

INDIA

MALAYSIA

LAYANG
LAYANG

THE PHILIPPINES

PACIFIC OCEAN

N

BORNEO

INDONESIA

INDIAN OCEAN

PAPUA
NEW GUINEA

AUSTRALIA

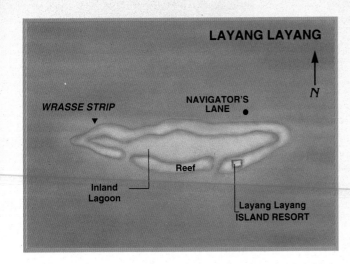

LAYANG LAYANG

WRASSE STRIP

NAVIGATOR'S LANE

N

Reef

Inland Lagoon

Layang Layang ISLAND RESORT

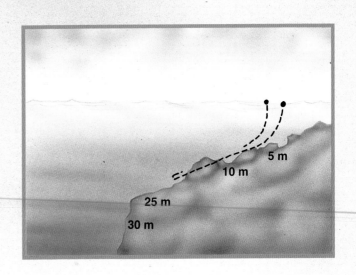

5 m

10 m

25 m

30 m

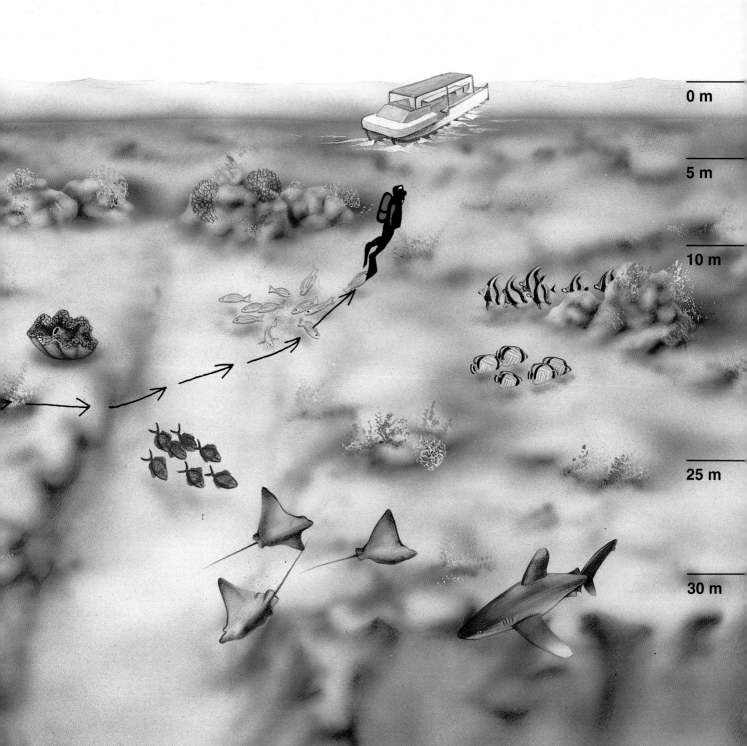

0 m

5 m

10 m

25 m

30 m

A dive at Wrasse Strip, like one at Navigator's Lane, a quite similar area, provides an unforgettable tour of one of the richest and most untouched coral reefs in the world. On a medium-to-deep dive here at over 30 meters in depth, it is possible to spot eagle rays, *Aetobatus narinari*, whitetip reef sharks, *Triaenodon obesus*, and sometimes even grey reef sharks, *Carcharhinus amblyrhynchos*. But the best part of Wrasse Strip is certainly from the surface to 20 meters deep, where the strong environmental light, heightened by the transparent waters of Layang Layang, permits a particularly rich and flourishing development of

C

A

B

D

corals. On the slope that gradually leads to the drop-off, there is an extraordinary concentration of pale, delicately colored soft and hard corals in large colonies, interrupted by small sandy flat areas and unexpected terraces facing the open sea.

This is the ideal environment for *Eretmochelys imbricata* turtles, which feed primarily on soft corals and sponges, and for manta rays, *Manta birostris*, which can sometimes be approached as they graze on the upper plankton layers. During the dive there are likely to be a few isolated whitetip reef sharks, *Triaenodon obesus*, small groups of batfish, *Platax*

orbicularis, great schools of surgeonfish from the genera *Naso* and *Acanthurus*, enormous concentrations of bluestripe seaperch, *Lutjanus kasmira*, numerous examples of saber squirrelfish, *Sargocentron spiniferum*, which are easy to approach, and *Plectorhynchus* grunts, immobile in the shade of the larger corals.

Careful observation of the seabed will be rewarded with finds like the vivid, fluorescent mantles of numerous giant clams in various species and tropical scorpionfish, *Scorpaenopsis barbata*, perfectly camouflaged among the detritus. Look out for the numerous "cleaning stations" along the way.

A - The excellent visibility that characterizes the seabeds of Layang Layang makes it possible to use extreme wide-angle lenses any time to achieve superb photographic effects.

B - The slope at medium depth is covered with soft corals, especially Xenia and Sarcophyton.

C - The plate Acropora formations which characterize the top reef at Wrasse Strip reach large dimensions.

Along the sandy flat areas that break the uniformity of the seabed are large schools of redtooth triggerfish, *Odonus niger*, ready to disappear among the coral cavities if a diver comes too close. Swarming around are butterflyfish, *Pomacanthus imperator* and *xanthometopon* angelfish, *Myripristis adusta* and *vittata* soldierfish, and crescent-tail bigeye, *Priacanthus hamrur*, as well as the numerous Moorish idols, *Zanclus cornutus*, which, rather rare in other areas, are present in large numbers on the reef of Layang Layang.
Divers should also watch for smaller creatures, which often have truly surprising colors and

G

H

E

F

forms. In fact, Wrasse Strip is the ideal location for admiring numerous species of lobster, *Palinurus argus* (unmistakable with its long, fragile antennae that protrude, oscillating, from its lair during the day), starfish (especially the rounded pincushion starfish, *Culcita novaguineae*, and the multicolored *Linckia laevigata*, with a certainly more orthodox form), nudibranchs (*Chromodoris, Phyllidia* and *Nembrotha*) and sea snails, as well as various species of minuscule blennies and crustaceans (carefully look among the branches of the hard corals of the genus *Pocillopora*).

G - The highly elegant Moorish idol, Zanclus comutas, *is quite common and easy to approach on all shallow seabeds of this splendid atoll.*

H - Extremely common elsewhere, the tasseled reef scorpionfish, Scorpaenopsis oxycephala, *is strangely rare in the waters of Layang Layang.*

D - Around dusk you may see dense groups of spotted sweetlips, Plectorhynchus chaetodonoides, *which gather in the shade of the coral formations.*

E - During April and May, Wrasse Strip is a good area to find large specimens of giant mantas, Manta birostris, *intently grazing on the superficial plankton layers.*

F - Along the reef of Wrasse Strip it is often possible to approach dense schools of yellow-tailed barracuda, Sphyraena flavicauda, *which do not exceed 40 centimeters in length.*

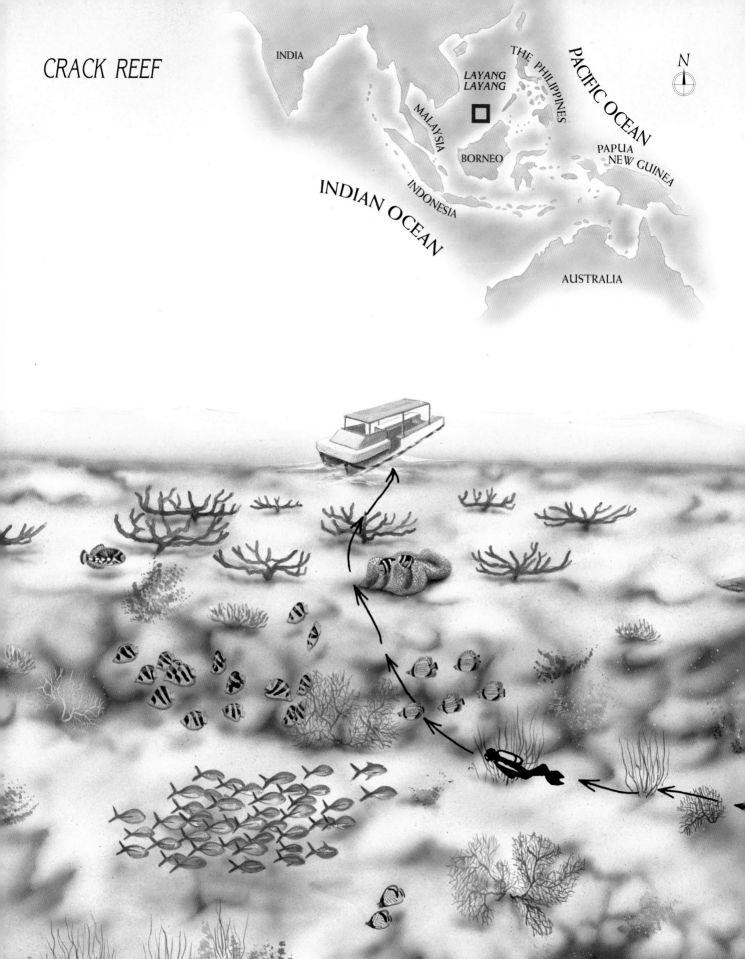

CRACK REEF

INDIA

LAYANG
LAYANG

THE PHILIPPINES

PACIFIC OCEAN

N

MALAYSIA

BORNEO

PAPUA
NEW GUINEA

INDONESIA

INDIAN OCEAN

AUSTRALIA

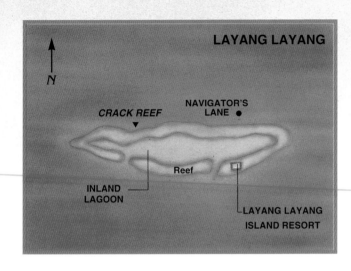

LAYANG LAYANG

N

CRACK REEF

NAVIGATOR'S
LANE

Reef

INLAND
LAGOON

LAYANG LAYANG
ISLAND RESORT

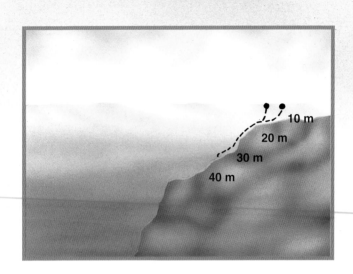

10 m

20 m

30 m

40 m

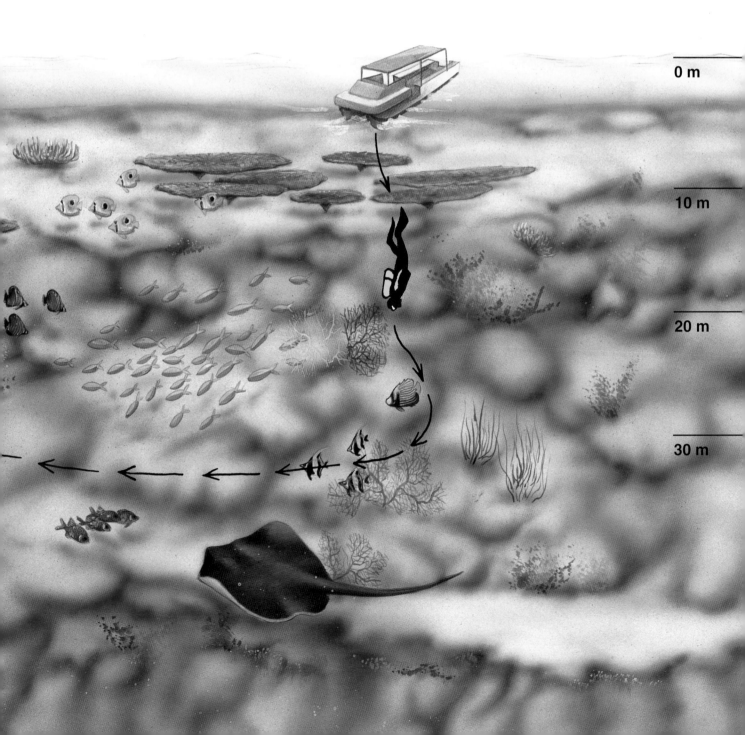

0 m

10 m

20 m

30 m

As the reef areas known as Crack Reef and Navigator's Lane, located along the northern side of the atoll, are immediately adjacent and virtually indistinguishable, we shall discuss them both in a single section. These are diving areas which are accessible even to less expert divers, and are characterized by a luxuriant coral garden located initially at a shallow depth, from five to15 meters, which then descends, first gradually and then more steeply, towards the unsounded depths that surround the atoll of Layang Layang. Although it is possible to make a fully satisfactory classical multi-level dive here (characterized by an initial brief downtime and then

A

a gradual diagonal ascent in stages to the customary safety stop near the surface), the sites are also splendid for a tranquil exploration entirely at medium or shallow depths, taking advantage of the extraordinary, untouched carpet of hard and soft corals and concentrating on the small but fascinating species which are inevitably ignored at sites full of spectacular encounters, such as The Point or Gorgonian Forest. Gently carried by the weak current, perhaps on a second or third dive of the day, divers can admire an astounding variety of species characteristic of the coral reef. Among the extremely fragile branches of *Acropora* are swarms of *Chaetodon* butterflyfish, coral

B

D

C

groupers, *Cephalopholis miniata*, and peacock groupers, *Cephalopholis argus*, *Plectorhynchus* grunts, *Myripristis vittata* and *adusta* squirrelfish and *Sargocentron spiniferum* soldierfish, while the more active triggerfish, *Odonus niger* and *Balistoides conspicillum* and *viridescens* dart everywhere, along with *Thalassoma* wrasses, small *Arothron* puffers and *Ostracion* boxfish, whose small size is more than offset by their garish and improbable colors. By stopping here and there and carefully observing the individual colonies of staghorn corals, it is not difficult to identify numerous brightly colored nudibranchs of various

A - The large gorgonians which protrude from the vertical walls of Layang Layang offer photographers excellent shots.

B - The extraordinary visibility that characterizes the seabeds of the atoll makes it possible to use fish-eye lenses with excellent results. Pictured here is an enormous yellow gorgonian fan.

C - At about 40 meters there are numerous gigantic colonies of black coral from the genus Antipatharia.

D - The large barrel sponges, Xestospongia testudinaria, host incredible forms of life on their surfaces and interiors.

E - Coral groupers are extremely numerous everywhere. This Cephalopholis leoparda is only 25 centimeters long and is one of the smaller species.

F - The filefish, Aluterus scriptus, is one of the most curious residents of the reef. This one sleeping among the corals is using the mimetic colors its adopts during periods of repose.

G - The royal angelfish, Pygoplites diacanthus, stands out for its elegance and bright colors.

H - This little pufferfish, Canthigaster valentini, resembles a precious enameled miniature more than a living creature.

species (Chromodoris, Phyllidia and Nembrotha), curious and uncommon sea snails, rare flatworms in the genus Pseudoceros with their characteristic undulating movements, tiny crustaceans that inhabit the corals and a large number of seabed residents usually difficult to spot, such as the peacock flounder, Bothus mancus, den gobies from the genus Amblyeleotris, firefish, Nemateleotris magnifica, and tiny coral gobies from the genus Bryaninops, with almost transparent bodies. Their characteristic undulating tentacles make it easy to identify the numerous large sea anemones, Radianthus and Stoichachtis. Also take note of their occasional "tenants", families of clown anemonefish from the genus Amphiprion, multi-hued shrimp from the genus Periclemenes, elegant porcelain crabs from the genus Neopetrolisthes, and much more rarely, large crayfish from the genus Saron, with extraordinary colors but strictly nocturnal habits. A little lower, where the reef overlooks the blue depths of the

G

H

South China Sea, swim large angelfish, Pomacanthus imperator, annularis, sextriatus and xanthometopon, regal angelfish, Pygoplites diacanthus, Moorish idols, Zanclus cornutus, turkeyfish, Pterois volitans, tropical scorpionfish from the genus Scorpaenopsis and, in the open water, large groups of pyramid butterflyfish, Hemitaurichthys polylepis, which are particularly characteristic of these waters, and fusiliers from the genus Caesio. If a deep dive is preferred, descend to about 40 meters, where a narrow little grotto opens, populated by an entire group of quite large turkeyfish, Pterois volitans.
Although the unexpected is always possible, these are two dives where an underwater photographer can still gain great satisfaction from using macro or even micro lenses.

E

F

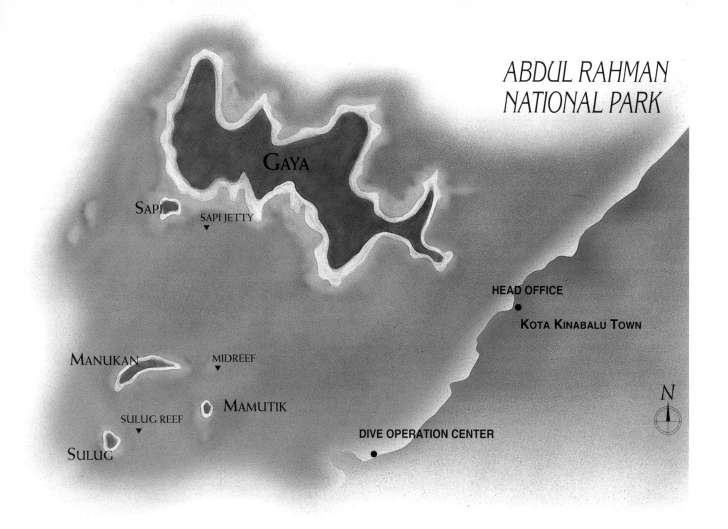

ABDUL RAHMAN NATIONAL PARK

GAYA

SAPI

SAPI JETTY ▾

HEAD OFFICE ●

KOTA KINABALU TOWN

MANUKAN

MIDREEF ▾

MAMUTIK

SULUG REEF ▾

SULUG

DIVE OPERATION CENTER ●

N

A - This spectacular panoramic photograph shows the splendid view of the Park as seen from the marina at Tanjung Aru Beach Hotel.

B - It is easy to spot large morays like this Gymnothorax javanicus *among the coral crevices that characterize the seabeds of Abdul Rahman.*

A

B

The capital of the state of Sabah in Borneo is the tranquil port city of Kota Kinabalu (known simply as "KK"), which is an inevitable intermediate stop between air transfers for Layang Layang, Pulau Sipadan or Pulau Mabul (for travelers on the mainland it is also the point of departure for the famous Mount Kinabalu). But this is also the departure point for one or more visits to the beautiful reefs of Tunku Abdul Rahman National Park, a spectacular marine sanctuary about 50 square kilometers in size created in 1974 in the waters directly opposite. The protected area includes the rich seabeds of the islands of Pulau Gaya and Pulau Sapi, as well as those of Pulau Manukan, Pulau Sulug and Pulau Mamutik: indeed, the five islands of the National Park form an elegant arc off the coast of Kota Kinabalu. Characterized by shallow waters and sumptuous coral gardens, the

area boasts splendid beaches and numerous, relatively sophisticated structures for visitors, which makes it an ideal weekend destination for local residents and a pleasant and unexpected alternative to city life for visitors forced to stay in Kota Kinabalu due to the unfathomable mysteries of air travel. It will take from 10-30 minutes of sailing to reach the Park, depending on the island and the type of boat selected. The boats of the Borneo Divers diving centers travel from the wharf of the elegant Tanjung Aru Beach Hotel, so that it is convenient to stay there for the night. It is always possible to rent complete gear for skin-diving or scuba-diving, and generally reservations are not needed far in advance. Pulau Gaya, with its 15 square kilometers of emerged surface area (with 21 kilometers of hiking trails that cross the forests and mangrove areas) is the largest of the five islands in the Tunku

Abdul Rahman Park. By following these paths it is easy to see herons, kingfishers, sea eagles and spectacular hornbills (the hornbill is the symbol of the state of Sabah).

Manukan is a bit smaller, and a good hiker can walk all the way around it in less than two hours. It has the best tourist facilities in the Park, with its bungalows managed by the Park Office of Sabah.

Sapi is little more than one kilometer long and only 200 meters wide, but along its five kilometers of hiking trails it is also possible to see various species of birds.

Pulau Mamutik is the closest to the mainland and is also the smallest - a triangle with sides only 250 meters long. Pulau Sulug, on the other hand, is the most distant, and is actually the only one in the Park that can boast a true drop-off, located at the end of a narrow tongue of sand jutting out into the blue of the open sea.

Reef microfauna can be seen everywhere - crabs, lobsters, multi-hued tropical mantis prawn, nudibranchs, cuttlefish, butterflyfish, pufferfish, boxfish and parrotfish, numerous species of scorpionfish, surgeonfish, rays, various species of morays, and above all the ever-present anemones with their vividly colored symbiotic clownfish and shrimp. Those who are more attentive and lucky may have the chance to admire rare antennarids, curious razorfish and the sinuous sea snake, *Laticauda colubrina*, which are present in great numbers especially in the waters of Pulau Tiga, a remote sanctuary located farther south. The opportunities for macro-photography are superb, but visibility is always rather poor given the proximity to the Borneo coast. The best period to visit the Park and dive in its waters is from March to October; from November to February weather conditions may make reaching the Park and diving there difficult. In any event, in order to dive here you must use a local diving center, where

C

E

F

resident instructors will know how to choose the most interesting locations. It is best to contact Borneo Divers (Wisma Sabah, Kota Kinabalu, tel. 222 226), which is historically the most reliable center and is also in charge of the largest and best resort on Pulau Sipadan.

C - During dives in the waters of the Park you can admire numerous sea anemones. Among their tentacles circle tiny symbiotic clownfish, such as the false clown anemonefish, Amphiprion ocellaris.

D - The reign of scorpionfish, the Park offers numerous ichthyic species, in particular the elegant turkeyfish, Pterois volitans.

E - Characteristic of murky waters, the graceful harp gorgonians, Ctenocella pectinata, *are numerous at Abdul Rahman.*

F - The waters of the Park offer exciting macrophotography opportunities. Here is a tiny pygmy goby from the genus Trimma.

SAPI JETTY

INDIA

THE PHILIPPINES

PACIFIC OCEAN

N

MALAYSIA

Abdul Rahman
National Park

BORNEO

INDONESIA

PAPUA
NEW GUINEA

INDIAN OCEAN

AUSTRALIA

0 m

1 m

6 m

ABDUL RAHMAN
NATIONAL PARK

N

GAYA

SAPI

SAPI
JETTY

HEAD OFFICE

MANUKAN

DIVE OPERATION
CENTER

SULUG

MAMUTIK

1 m

6 m

A

A - In the waters of the Park it is sometimes possible to approach the fascinating but poisonous striped sea snake, Laticauda colubrina.

B - The sandy seabed at the base of the jetty hosts schools of tiny immature striped catfish, Plotosus lineatus.

C - This close-up shows the poisonous but non-aggressive striped sea snake, Laticauda colubrina.

D - Numerous interesting members of the Monocanthidae family like this Acreichthys tomentosum often find refuge among the piles of the jetty.

E - Immature batfish, Platax teira, seem to greatly appreciate the shelter offered by the Sapi jetty.

F - The elegant colors of a cardinal fish from the genus Apogon stand out on the background of the multicolored sponges that encrust the piles of the jetty.

G - The sandy slope at the base of the jetty offers a rare opportunity to observe numerous gobies. The photograph shows a lemon goby, Cryptocentrus cinctus. Note its elegant coloring.

H - Another fascinating inhabitant of the sandy seabed of Sapi Jetty is the multicolored dragonet, Dactylopus dactylopus.

Against the panoramic background of the idyllic rain forest-covered slopes of Pulau Gaya and Pulau Sapi, the long wooden jetty on the latter island juts out from an immaculate beach toward the blue-green channel separating the two islands.

Divers leave the shade of the rain forest, from which macaws and hornbills peer out curiously, and slide gently into the water from the beach, onto a sandy slope at a depth that varies from 50 centimeters to six meters. Visibility is little more than mediocre, but this is not a problem, as the first part of the dive will be devoted to the myriad

E

of creatures that populate the sandy seabed. In just a few minutes it is possible to see numerous yellow shrimp gobies, *Cryptocentrus cinctus*, which peep out of the lairs they share with shrimp from the genus *Alpheus*, as well as so-called "tricky Nicki", *Trichonotus setigerus*, eel-shaped fish about 30 centimeters long which rapidly bury themselves in the sand, sea anemones with their symbiont clownfish and shrimp, spotted stingrays (especially from the species *Dasyatis kuhlii*) and panther flounder, *Bothus pantherinus*. Also visible may be the splendid dragonets, *Dactylopus dactylopus*, characteristic of sandy seabeds, and a few young individuals from the genus *Platax orbicularis*, perfectly camouflaged by dead leaves with their brown and seemingly rough skin. As divers proceed slowly and carefully to avoid raising clouds of annoying suspended particles, they may observe numerous pipefish and, lower down, large cuttlefish, *Sepia pharaonis*, which can reach one meter in length and are quite easy to approach. If they watch the surface from below, they may also see "squadrons" of squid, *Sepioteuthis lessoniana*, in perfect, bioluminescent formation. Proceeding in a wide semicircle, they then begin their return to the jetty (watch out for the motorboats coming and going just a few meters above).

Here and there are small coral formations (especially *Acropora*) visibly stressed and damaged by the muddy sedimentation. In them live small crustaceans, as well as a few perfectly camouflaged large stonefish, *Synanceia verrucosa*.

The dive ends right below the wooden piles of the Sapi jetty, which are splendidly encrusted with a great variety of sponges in every color, mollusks and festoons of brightly colored algae. As often occurs in these situations, the man-made structure has to some extent ended up becoming an oasis, offering refuge and protection for a myriad of very interesting species. Among the clouds of vividly colored *Apogon* cardinal fish, restless *Monacanthidae* with their superbly mimetic coloring and nearly spherical schools of poisonous striped catfish, *Plotosus lineatus*, it will not be difficult to spot the waving white antennae of the cleaner shrimp, *Stenopus hispidus*, the monstrous form of a large stonefish, *Synanceia verrucosa*, the silvery barbels of a group of young batfish, *Platax teira*, and, with a bit of luck, the sinuous and fascinating movement of a striped sea snake, *Laticauda colubrina*, a deadly poisonous reptile, which is fortunately not at all aggressive.

F

G

H

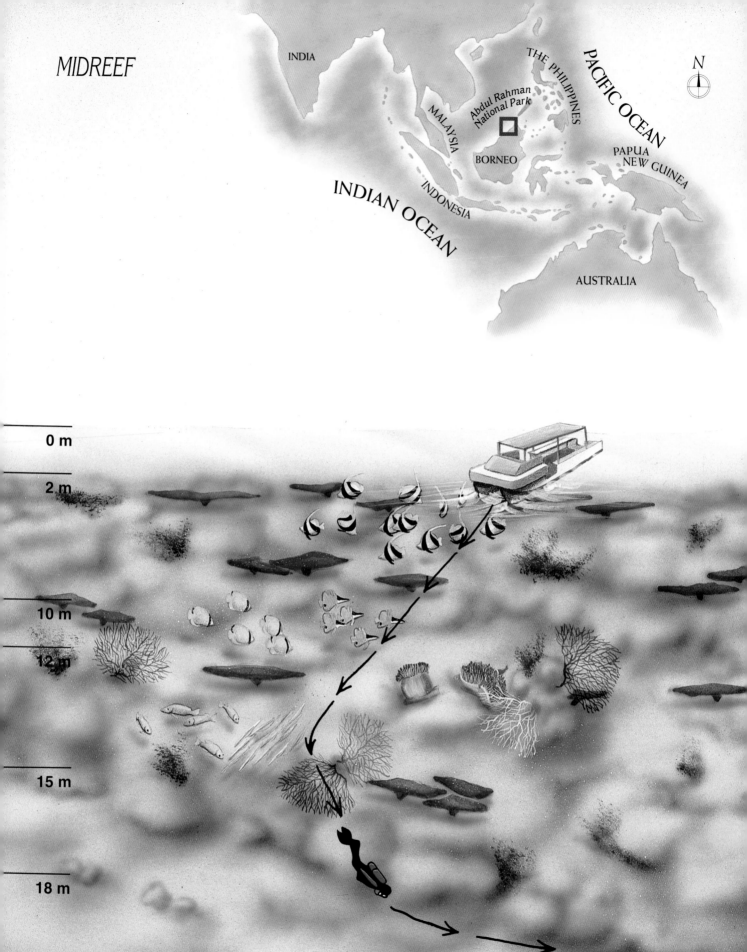

MIDREEF

INDIA
THE PHILIPPINES
PACIFIC OCEAN
MALAYSIA
Abdul Rahman
National Park
BORNEO
PAPUA
NEW GUINEA
INDONESIA
INDIAN OCEAN
AUSTRALIA
N

0 m
2 m
10 m
12 m
15 m
18 m

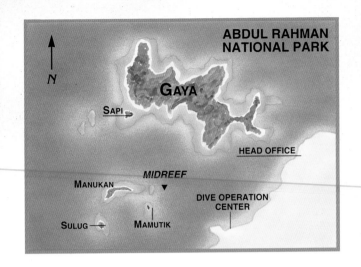

ABDUL RAHMAN
NATIONAL PARK

GAYA

N

SAPI

HEAD OFFICE

MIDREEF

MANUKAN

DIVE OPERATION
CENTER

SULUG   MAMUTIK

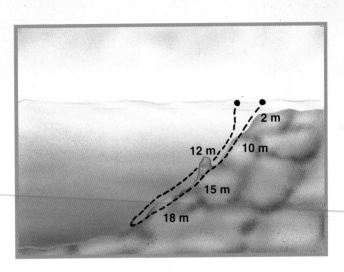

2 m

12 m   10 m

15 m

18 m

The submerged coral reef at Midreef is basically in the form of a flat cupola that rises from the surrounding sandy seabeds. As in many other areas in Tunku Abdul Rahman, it is hard to appreciate it fully due to the dense veil of suspended plankton that characterizes this arm of the sea.

After taking advantage of the descent down the long slope of the reef to observe its various inhabitants (in particular, anemones with their symbiont clownfish and shrimp, small groups of razorfish, *Aeoliscus strigatus*, and numerous species of butterflyfish, including the lovely *Chelmon rostratus*, characteristic

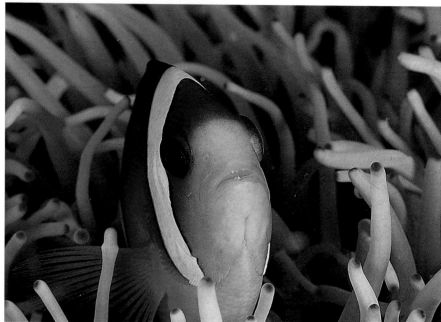

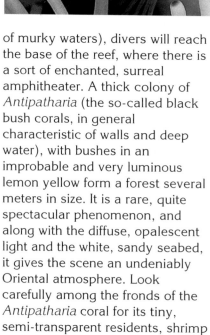

A - A family of clownfish, Amphiprion ocellaris, *with their brilliant orange colors, peers out of an anemone.*

B - A colorful gorgonian of an unidentified species offers a comfortable resting place for a crinoid.

C - The seabed at Midreef hosts numerous colonies of seawhip gorgonians.

D - This photograph shows the snout of a timid Clark's anemonefish, Amphiprion clarkii, *as it curiously pokes out of the tentacles of an anemone.*

of murky waters), divers will reach the base of the reef, where there is a sort of enchanted, surreal amphitheater. A thick colony of *Antipatharia* (the so-called black bush corals, in general characteristic of walls and deep water), with bushes in an improbable and very luminous lemon yellow form a forest several meters in size. It is a rare, quite spectacular phenomenon, and along with the diffuse, opalescent light and the white, sandy seabed, it gives the scene an undeniably Oriental atmosphere. Look carefully among the fronds of the *Antipatharia* coral for its tiny, semi-transparent residents, shrimp and cardinalfish.

Also prevalent are the true lords of these seabeds, the large tropical cuttlefish, *Sepia pharaonis*, massive, peaceful cephalopods which can reach a meter in length and several kilograms in weight, which gather here in great numbers during the reproduction season. They constantly change the color and "finishing touches" of their superficial tissues depending on their mood.

When approached calmly and cautiously, the cuttlefish seem willing to interact with divers - an opportunity quite rare in other waters. The wise and somewhat alien eyes of these intelligent mollusks follow the diver attentively as they observe them at close range. (It is hard to resist the feeling that the cuttlefish is trying to communicate with you, as it alternates from fear and caution to unrestrained curiosity.) It is important to move slowly, approaching the cephalopods calmly, and to make absolutely no attempt to touch them. They may come almost close enough to touch divers, their mantle changing frenetically in a confusion of luminous and chromatic signals.

Midreef is certainly not the only diving site in Borneo where divers can experience these encounters - the giant tropical cuttlefish are rather common in the more sheltered coastal areas at shallow

E

depths - but this is certainly the easiest place to visit them. During a single dive, it is not uncommon to encounter seven or eight of these mysterious and fascinating creatures, which are clearly animated by the same speculative intelligence that divers have also learned to recognize in the common octopus.

Given the shallow depth, the ascent will take only a few minutes, and a safety stop can be enjoyed near the upper portions of the reef before returning to the boat.

F
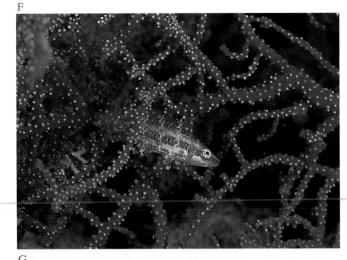

G

H

I
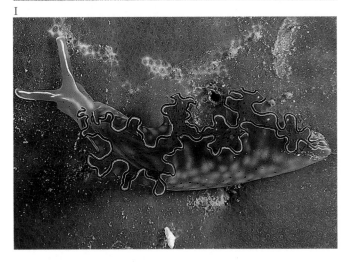

E - An encounter with a gigantic cuttlefish, Sepia pharaonis, shown here in a threatening pose, is one of the most interesting opportunities offered by Midreef.

F - A tiny wrasse from the genus Cheilinus is effectively camouflaged among the branches of a red gorgonian.

G - On the seabeds of Tunku Abdul Rahman it is easy to observe the elegant striped cleaner shrimp, Stenopus hispidus.

H - If you move calmly and delicately you can almost touch the large tropical cuttlefish. This photograph shows the eye of one superb specimen.

I - A sea snail from the genus Elysia, with its rather odd coloring, is not at all intimidated by the photographer.

SULUG REEF

INDIA

MALAYSIA

Abdul Rahman
National Park

THE PHILIPPINES

PACIFIC
OCEAN

N

BORNEO

INDONESIA

PAPUA
NEW GUINEA

INDIAN OCEAN

AUSTRALIA

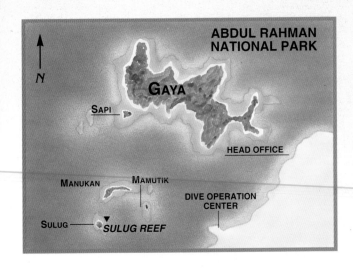

ABDUL RAHMAN
NATIONAL PARK

N

GAYA

SAPI

HEAD OFFICE

MANUKAN   MAMUTIK

SULUG   SULUG REEF

DIVE OPERATION
CENTER

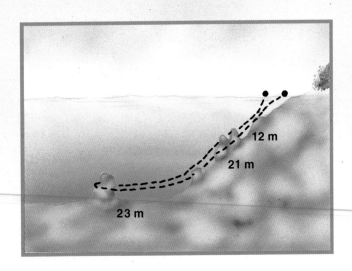

12 m

21 m

23 m

0 m

12 m

21 m

23 m

The top reef of Sulug where this dive takes place is invisible most of the time because of the great quantity of suspended particles. This is not a great loss, however, because the top reef is in reality composed of mostly detrital material and dead coral. If divers continue to descend along the gentle slope, visibility gradually improves.

On reaching the sandy seabed at a depth of about 25 meters, they should linger for a few minutes near a strange point of interest: an artificial microreef composed of large tires, a curious testimony to how underwater life tends to exploit every niche available. Among the tires are many beautiful, surprisingly large nudibranchs - in Tunku Abdul Rahman National Park it is not uncommon to see nudibranchs from the genus *Phyllidia* as long as 10 centimeters.

Also visible are swarms of cleaner shrimp (especially the insignificant transparent *Periclemenes*, but in the darker corners of the mass are

A - There are numerous colorful sponges on the seabeds of Sulug. Their colors are set off by the light of the camera flash.

B - By going deeper, you can admire splendid colonies of whip gorgonians from the genus Elisella, which become a brilliant red under artificial light.

C - On the top reef of Sulug there are numerous multicolored crinoids from the genera Comanthina and Lamprometra, which can reach extremely large dimensions.

D - A jewel in the rubbish: this marvelous sea slug from the genus Chromodoris shines on a pile of old tires.

E - Spotted-faced morays, Gymnothorax fimbriatus, are easy to see in the cracks of the reef.

F - A multicolored spiny devilfish, Inimicus didactylus, hovers permanently near the submerged stack at Sulug.

crowds of beautiful *Lysmata amboinensis* and *Stenopus hispidus*), gobies, morays, small scorpionfish, *Dendrochirus brachypterus* and *Dendrochirus zebra*, and many large, odd-looking albino pipefish, or at least white pipefish which apparently have not yet been classified.

Continuing at the same depth and keeping the base of the reef to their left, divers will reach a single stack of rocks emerging from the sand after a few dozen meters. Despite its small size - it is no more than 1.8 meters tall - it is literally covered with a large quantity of sessile organisms, which in their turn host entire animal communities.

Among the "branches" of the large gorgonians and soft corals it easy to identify numerous cleaner shrimp from the genus *Periclemenes* and other species, while all around swim clouds of cardinalfish from the genus *Apogon*. At the foot of the block of rock, perfectly camouflaged in the sandy substratum, may be various specimens of reef scorpionfish, *Scorpaenopsis venosa*, and devil scorpionfish, *Inimicus didactylus*. Watch out for the latter, perhaps the most grotesque of all scorpionfish. It has long, disorderly dorsal spines and is almost always lying in wait half-buried in the sand, from which only its eyes and prognathic mouth protrude. If disturbed it does not hesitate to unfold its spectacular pectoral fins with their impressive, beautiful warning coloration.

The dive continues with a slow diagonal ascent to conclude in a pleasant coral garden characterized by large terraces of *Acropora* and a rich sedentary fauna typical of the reef. While ascending, it will not be difficult to spot a few large, friendly specimens of the giant tropical cuttlefish, *Sepia pharaonis*, or an elegant moray, *Gymnothorax flavimarginata*, to finish off that last roll of film.

As in all dives in the waters of Tunku Abdul Rahman, at Sulug divers should move with extreme care to avoid needlessly raising annoying clouds of suspended particles and making the already limited visibility even worse.

D

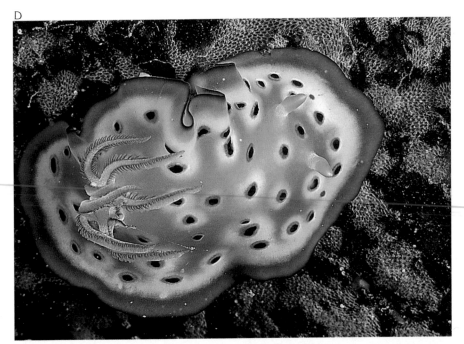

E

F

THE LABUAN WRECKS

A

B

The map shows LABUAN with MARINA marked, DAAT to the east, CEMENT WRECK and KURAMAN to the southwest, RUSUKAN KECHIL and RUSUKAN BESAR further south.

N

The island of Labuan is located 115 kilometers south of Kota Kinabalu and about eight kilometers off the coast of Sabah, near the mouth of the Bay of Brunei. Labuan is an important maritime city and port, as well as an major collecting center for the Malaysian mining industries located on the seabeds of the South China Sea.

As a free port, it has also been declared an International Offshore Financial Center for Malaysia. Its history, which has always been intimately bound to that of maritime traffic, began over three centuries ago with the first commercial transactions between Chinese junks and the Sultanate of Brunei. During the last century the island was also utilized by English steamers as a supply station and fuel depot.

This colonial period was also the romantic and cruel era of James Brooke, the "white rajah of Sarawak", who inspired Emilio Salgari in his saga of *The Tigers of Malaysia*. More recently, during

C

D

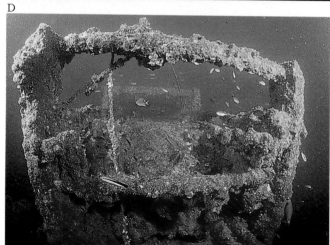

A - Several of the wrecks at Labuan are characterized by a large quantity of brightly colored alcyonarians form the genus Dendronephthya. Photograph by Michael Aw/ Borneo Divers

B - Schools of large sweetlips often hover among the now deformed structures of the wrecks. Photograph by Michael Aw/ Borneo Divers

C - A degree of experience and the collaboration of an expert divemaster are necessary to explore the internal structures of the Labuan wrecks. Photograph by Michael Aw/ Borneo Divers

World War II, Labuan was the scene of bitter conflicts between the Japanese and Allied air and naval forces, and the wrecks for which Labuan is now known and appreciated by international diving circles in fact date back to this period.

Of the four wrecks which have been identified to date and can be visited, two are ships sunk during the last World War (the other two, the Philippine fishing boat *Mabini Padre* and the motorship *Tung Hwang*, date to the 1980s). These are dives accessible to anyone, although exploration of the internal structures is advisable for experts only.

In any event, if you want to visit the wrecks, you should contact the Labuan headquarters of Borneo Divers (Labuan Marina Centre, tel: 60-87 41587), a PADI center with comfortable motorboats equipped with GPS and echolocators. As we have noted, to date four wrecks have been identified, but in the future the shallow waters around Labuan could reveal the hulk of an

American P-40 Warhawk or a Japanese Zero. For the moment it is possible to explore the so-called "American wreck" (the American minesweeper, the *USS Salute,* built in 1943 and sunk after a brief but glorious career as the result of a collision with a Japanese mine during the Allied landing on Borneo on June 8, 1945), the so-called "Australian wreck" (in reality a Dutch armed cargo ship captured in Indonesia by the Japanese forces in 1942 and sunk in 1945, presumably following a collision with a mine), the "cement wreck" (the cargo ship *Tung Hwang*, sunk under unclear circumstances with its cargo of cement destined for the Brunei building yards) and the "open sea wreck" (the Philippine fishing boat *Mabini Padre*, sunk on November 13, 1981 northeast of the island of Kuraman following a fire on board which went out of control: its nickname comes from its distance of 35 kilometers from Labuan). All four are large wrecks (the *Tung Hwang* is 92 meters long) located at accessible depths

G - Green sea turtles, Chelonia mydas, are not uncommon in the waters of Labuan.

G

H

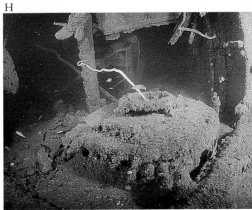

(20-40 meters). The only problem for divers - actually more for photographers - is visibility, which is generally fair and often poor (from six to 20 meters) and can vary greatly from day to day. To avoid disappointment, it is best to visit the Labuan wrecks in the middle of the dry season, when suspended particles and detritus from the mainland and estuaries are at a minimum.

D - An extreme wide-angle lens should be used wherever possible to photograph the external structures of the wrecks. Photograph by Michael Aw/ Borneo Divers

E - The remains of the Labuan wrecks host a large number of poisonous scorpionfish like this tasseled reef scorpionfish, Scorpaenopsis oxycephala.

F - A careful observation of the wreck reveals a moray peeping curiously out of the lair in which it is hiding.

E

F

H - Fans of underwater wrecks will find numerous points of interest in the waters of Labuan, mostly *ships sunk during the World War II.* Photograph by Michael Aw/ Borneo Divers

CEMENT WRECK

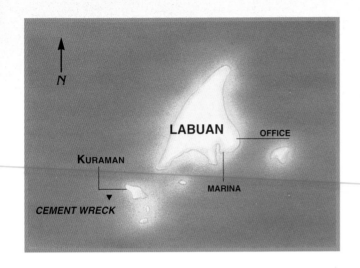

LABUAN

OFFICE

KURAMAN

MARINA

CEMENT WRECK

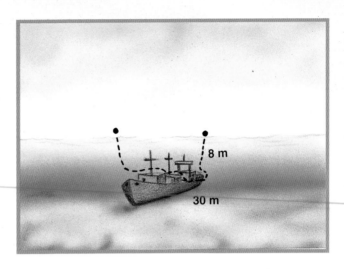

8 m

30 m

0 m

8 m

30 m

The remains of the cargo motorship *Tung Hwang*, nicknamed the "cement wreck", rests in sailing position on a sandy seabed 30 meters deep about 20 kilometers from Labuan, east of the island of Kuraman. The 25 meter-long ship sank on September 25, 1980 after a collision with the Bank of Samarang caused it irreparable damage. Its year of construction is still unknown.
At the time of the tragedy it was transporting a cargo of cement to the building yards of the new palace of the Sultan of Brunei. Accounts of the disaster vary: some say that the ship sank before arriving at its destination,

C

A - The remains of the masts of the motorship Tung Hwang are wreathed by lush, multicolored colonies of alcyonarians from the genus Dendonephthya. Photograph by Michael Aw/ Borneo Divers

B - The use of an extreme wide-angle lens makes it possible to obtain excellent seascape photos of the wreck of the Tung Hwang. Photograph by Michael Aw/ Borneo Divers

C - The broadsides of the cargo ship, which sank on September 25, 1980, are now entirely covered with multicolored concretions.

D - The photograph shows another example of the delicate colors characteristic of the soft corals that cover the wreck of the Tung Hwang. Photograph by Michael Aw/ Borneo Divers

A

D

B

while others assert that it sank during the return voyage, after the cargo, apparently of poor quality, had been refused by its recipient. In any event, the crew was rescued by local fishing boats. Due to the wreck's position (the masts are only eight meters deep, with the roof of the steerage area at 14 meters and the main bridge at 18 meters), this wreck is the easiest to explore of the four wrecks near Labuan, and the abundant life that covers it definitely makes it the most photogenic.
Large schools of trevallies, barracuda, fusiliers from the genus *Caesio*, batfish from the genus *Platax* and numerous large

groupers incessantly patrol the masts, bridges and hull, while the great bulkheads are almost entirely covered with a multi-hued carpet of brilliant alcyonarians from the genus *Dendronephtya*, some of which are up to one meter long. Everywhere crinoids stretch into the current, with large colonies of black corals and sea anemones. Sheltered by the large, partially collapsed smokestack are numerous *Pterois volitans*, or turkeyfish, some of which are unusually large, clouds of cardinalfish and large sponges. It is also not uncommon to see *Chelonia mydas* and *Eretmochelys imbricata* turtles

E - The dwarf hawkfish, Cirrhitichthys falco, is a small, active predator characteristic of the surface areas of the coral reef.

F - The Labuan wrecks are the reign of scorpionfish. The most photogenic and spectacular is probably the graceful turkeyfish, Pterois volitans.

G - On the detrital seabed there are numerous small lizardfish from the genus Saurida, *characterized by their sharp teeth exposed in a permanent leer.*

H - In the darker corners of the wreck there are often groups of nocturnal shrimp, Rhynchocinetes uritai, *whose bright colors are set off by the camera flash.*

I - It is easy to spot numerous small white-eyed morays, Syderea thyrsoidea, *among the rubble of the ships.* Photograph by Michael Aw/ Borneo Divers

E

F

G

H

passing by. This area offers many opportunities for macrophotography buffs, although, visibility permitting, there are also shots for those who prefer medium and extreme wide-angle lenses, with photos enlivened by the vivid colors of the sessile fauna that has encrusted the motorship's superstructures.
Divers with a degree of experience in exploring wrecks and the necessary equipment (a torch is sufficient in this case) can accompany the divemaster inside the hold, the bunks and the machine room.
Dives outside the wreck are extremely easy and accessible to

I

anyone, and are perhaps preferable for underwater photographers.
One word of warning: as with all wrecks on fishing routes, be careful not to get entangled in the fishing lines and nets that envelop the large superstructures like a floating shroud.

DIVES IN PENINSULAR MALAYSIA

It would clearly be impossible to describe each individual diving area in Malaysia which deserves to be included in this guide with all the details we have included up to now. Those described on the preceding pages are simply the areas which, due to their isolated position and unique features, have proven particularly worthy of the international fame they enjoy with demanding divers. It is true that visiting them and diving on their seabeds may involve long and costly trips, especially for Western tourists. But it would be wrong to believe that the only diving areas in Malaysia worthy of note are those we have discussed up to now. There are numerous others which are easier to reach and often have greater comforts, so that you can visit them as part of a classical vacation on dry land, perhaps in the company of friends who prefer the beach to

A - The shallower areas of less disturbed Malaysian coral reefs are characterized by large schools of purple anthias, Pseudanthias tuka.

B - The drop-offs and diving areas farther away from the coast host large concentrations of pelagic fauna, like these bigeye trevallies, Caranx sexfasciatus.

C - There are numerous opportunities for macrophotography everywhere. This picture shows a rare harlequin ghost pipefish, Solenostomus ornatus, appearing to be pose for the photographer.

A

C

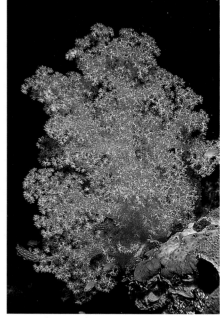

B

underwater exploration. Of course, these areas do not always offer the unique environmental conditions and richness of species of the sites we have discussed above, but they are nevertheless very beautiful areas both on land and underwater, full of microfauna and coral formations and ideal for a totally relaxing vacation.

PULAU PERENTHIAN

The islands with the most developed tourist facilities in all Malaysia are along the eastern coast. As this area is affected by monsoons during the winter, the ideal season to visit them is from March to October. Among the most popular areas is the Perhentian group, near the northern border of Thailand, marked by the two islands of Pulau Perhentian Besar and Pulau Perhentian Kecil. They are separated by a navigable channel

E

F

D

G

H

running north to south. The only village, Kampung Pasir Hantu, is on the southeast point of the latter island, where visitors can stay in comfortable and romantic native-style bungalows. The surrounding seabeds are generally well-developed and at shallow depth. They offer splendid opportunities for macro-photography, but large representatives of pelagic fauna, including whale sharks or mantas, may also be encountered.
To dive, you should contact local diving centers or the diving centers of Kuala Terengganu, the starting point for reaching the islands. The area, like those which follow, has been declared a Marine Park.

D - The soft corals from the genus Dendronephthya *add delicate colors to the Malaysian seabeds, especially in areas where the current is stronger.*

E - The large barrel sponges, Xestospongia testudinaria, *grow to great size but are limited to the deeper seabeds.*

F - The drop-offs and walls of the Malaysian islands often offer scenes of great beauty. This photo shows an exceptionally large gorgonian.

G - A tiny pixy hawkfish, Oxycirrhites typus, *lies in wait among the branches of a black coral from the genus* Antipatharia.

H - This goby, Bryaninops loki, *is resting on the branches of a gorgonian from the genus* Elisella.

PULAU REDANG

A - The photograph shows the lush seabed that characterizes Pulau Redang. Note in particular the large colonies of Acropora and Porites that host numerous multicolored coral fish.

B - An encounter with a silvery wall of barracuda is always thrilling.

C - A diver observes several fans of yellow gorgonians which have become quite lush due to the current that transports large qualities of plankton and microorganisms.

The Pulau Redang group is probably the preferred destination for Malaysian divers. Consisting of nine islands, this small archipelago boasts a native village, Kampung Redang, located on the estuary of the River Redang. To the south is the island of Pulau Pinang, while along the eastern coast are the islands of Palau Lima, Pulau Paku Besar and Pulau Paku Kecil, Pulau Kerengga Kecil, Pulau Kerengga Besar and Pulau Ekor Tebu. All have well-developed coral gardens at shallow depths, with large colonies of Acropora and Porites and an extremely diverse representation of classic sedentary reef fauna. Redang is an ideal place to combine diving activities (either with scuba gear or by simply snorkeling) with a relaxing beach vacation. In any event, don't underestimate the excellent photo opportunities offered by the numerous species on these

C

A

B

D

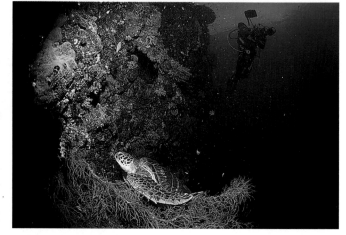

seabeds, especially for macrophotography, although encounters with turtles are also not uncommon. At present it is not possible to spend the night on Redang, so the best thing to do is contact a diving center on Kuala Terengganu to organize a trip to the island.

D - During dives at Pulau Redang, it is not rare to encounter extraordinary specimens of sea turtles. The one pictured here, which seems to want to flee from the photographer, has taken refuge near a gorgonian sea fan.

PULAU TENGGOL

E - The large Boers batfish, Platax boersii, *is perhaps the most elegant member of the batfish family.*

F - Along the coral wall of Sulug you can observe numerous splendid examples of giant cuttlefish, Sepia pharaonis.

G - The saber squirrelfish, Sargocentrum spiniferum, *is a very common predator characteristic of the shallower areas of the reef.*

H - The ever-present bistred hawkfish, Paracirrhites arcuatus, *is a tiny and unmistakable predator which is rather difficult to approach.*

H - Characteristic of detrital seabeds at shallow depths, the tiny mandarin fish, Synchiropus splendidus, *is one of the most timid and colorful inhabitants of the reef.*

This is another small island off the coat of the state of Terengganu, which, with its multitudes of easily accessible coral seabeds, is a paradise for Malaysian divers.

The rocky seabeds of Pulau Tenggol offer stretches of still untouched coral reef, where exciting encounters are common. Photographers will also find numerous points of great interest on dry land, as in all the other Malaysian islands.

Indeed, unlike the exclusive destinations of demanding divers, such as Layang Layang or Sipadan, the islands off the eastern coast are characterized by spectacular landscapes (rivers, deserted beaches, mangroves and dense tropical forests) and numerous areas of ethnic interest (for example, you can visit a *kampung,* or coastal fishing village, but remember not to be invasive, and to ask permission before you take photographs).

PULAU TIOMAN

ome say that Pulau Tioman is the most beautiful island in the world. Certainly, few other areas can boast such a spectacular variety of natural environments - deserted beaches, tropical forests, rivers and streams and picturesque fishing villages (the most popular ones are Tekek and Kampung Salang). The coral seabeds of the island of Tioman itself have suffered much over recent years due to excessive human impact - the island is one of the major tourist destinations in Malaysia - and due to the rapacious incursions of the crown-of-thorns starfish, *Acanthaster plancii*, which can devour wide stretches of reef in a short time. Nevertheless, for those staying on the island it is not difficult to organize excursions with local diving centers to neighboring islands, which along with Tioman are part of the Pahang Marine Park. The most interesting for diving purposes are Pulau Chebeh, Pulau Tulai and Pulau Labas; closer to the mainland are also Pulau Babi Tengah, Pulau Babi Hujung and Pulau Rawa.
Here as well, gardens of *Acropora* are common, along with vigorous colonies of alcyonarians, various species of wrasse, butterflyfish from the genus *Chaetodon* and various species of large tropical sea anemones with their clownfish from the genus *Amphiprion*.
For photography buffs, the use of medium lenses is recommended for portraits of reef fauna (such as the 35mm Nikonos or a 24-50mm zoom for those who use underwater reflex cameras) or macro photos, with many excellent shots possible. Pulau Tioman and the surrounding islands are within the jurisdiction of the state of Pahang, although in general those who reach the island via sea set out from the coastal city of Mersing, in the state of Johore. This later port also offers the possibility of reaching good seabeds with lovely coral reefs near the islands of Pulau Aur, Pulau

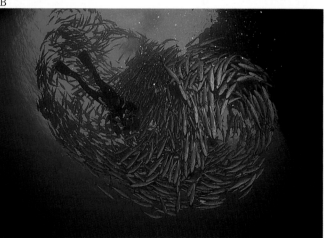

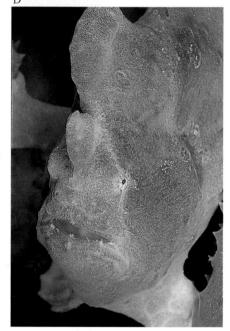

Pemanggil and Pulau Dayang. Nevertheless, Western visitors usually reach Pulau Tioman by air. Indeed, the island's great development as a tourist area, with hotel structures ranging from rustic bungalows to five-star hotels, guarantees it convenient daily connections to Kuala Lumpur and Singapore (about a one-hour flight).

A - The rich coral seabeds of Pulau Tioman are being threatened by the crown-of-thorns starfish, Acanthaster planci, which can destroy long stretches of reef within a short time.

B - In order to better observe a group of barracuda, a diver swims within the vortex which these silvery fish often form.

C - Crinoids are primitive but extremely interesting inhabitants and can easily be observed along all the Malaysian coral reefs.

D - Frogfish are predators with curious habits. They are very difficult to identify on the reef due to their excellent mimetic skills.

PULAU LANGKAWI

G

H

S ituated near the Thailand border, off its western coast, the large island of Langkawi, in the Andaman Sea, rivals Pulau Tioman as the number-one tourist attraction for Western visitors. Famous worldwide for its splendid beaches, luxurious hotels and the legendary tale of the Princess Mahsuri, Pulau Langkawi nevertheless suffers from a serious defect, as far as divers are concerned: its great mass results in the discharge of large amounts of fresh water into the sea, which alters the salinity of the superficial layers of the surrounding waters, greatly limiting the development of coral formations. Its proximity to the mainland (Langkawi is only 35 kilometers from the coast) only makes the situation worse. However, those who want to spend their vacation on Langkawi can organize one or more

E - Clownfish, like these Amphiprion ocellaris, *and the anemones which host them, are easily observable in any of the diving sites in Malaysia and Borneo.*

F - Because of their innate elegance, batfish are a preferred subject for photographers.

G - Alcyonarians are at their maximum splendor when they become swollen in the currents.

H - A careful examination among the pinnules of a crinoid will reveal symbiotic shrimp from the genus Periclemenes, *with their astounding mimetic skills.*

E

F

excursions with a local diving center to the Marine Park of the Segantang islands, located halfway between Pulau Langkawi and Penang (another popular tourist attraction). The islands which comprise the group - Pulau Segantang, Pulau Paya, Pulau Lembu and Pulau Kaca - have some of the few coral reefs worthy of note on the western coast, a good representation of marine fauna (more characteristic of the Indian Ocean or the Andaman Sea than the Malaysian seas) and, above all, excellent diving visibility due to their distance from the coast and the murky waters of the Strait of Malacca.

Between February and April, the boom in plankton in these areas attracts large pelagic filtering species such as mantas and whale sharks which divers may be lucky enough to encounter.

LIFE ON THE MALAYSIAN SEABEDS

Some of the most diverse marine areas on our planet are located around the Malaysian peninsula - that point of the mainland that breaks away from the Asian continent, wedging itself between the South China Sea and the Strait of Malacca - and the northern part of the large island of Borneo. These Malaysian seas include coastal and island reefs, rocks and beaches and wide expanses of shallow seabeds broken by ocean trenches over 2,000 meters deep, creating a mosaic of environmental conditions. For instance, the current may cloud the transparent waters a month earlier than usual, carrying in large amounts of plankton, and the seasonal rains can make dives in the coastal waters unappealing. As it is absolutely impossible to summarize the marine fauna, extremely rich almost everywhere, it is better to respect its diversity. Pulau Sipadan is considered one of the most beautiful areas to dive, and it is probably the most famous of these seas. Its name in the local language means "boundary island", which seems to be an implicit recognition of its proximity to so many different environments. Sipadan is the top of a volcanic cone that rises from a depth of 600 meters to emerge just a few meters above the surface, and is thickly covered with luxuriant vegetation that offers shelter for dozens of species of birds and numerous coconut crabs *(Birgis latro)*. Along the coast of the island and easily accessible, over 200 species of fish and about 70 species of corals in the most varied shapes and forms imaginable have been found. The umbrellas of plate *Acropora* mingle with the rounded scales of the lettuce corals and the formations of the brain corals. Among these are giant clams, soft and leather corals, sponges and gorgonians, which in their turn become suitable substrata for oysters, vertebrates, sea squirts, sea slugs, sea urchins, starfish and yellow and black crinoids with plumed arms extended into the currents. From the beach to the summit of the inner reef, as well as along the outside walls which in some points plunge toward the volcanic abyss, there are fish of all sizes. Small lagoon blennies and gobies, sometimes accompanied by scavenger shrimp, defend their territory from young angelfish and butterflyfish, which mingle with lionfish, surgeonfish, triggerfish, damselfish and goatfish. Beyond the breakers there are dense schools of sergeant majors, anthias, damselfish, Ray's breams, moon wrasses and angelfish. Just a few meters from the reef live numerous fusiliers *(Caesio teres* and *C. lunaris)* searching for plankton, spadefish *(Platax* sp.), unicornfish *(Naso* sp.) and Moorish idols *(Zanclus cornutus)*, among which silvery bigeye trevallies make rapid incursions. The greater depths are occupied by colored clown triggerfish *(Balistoides conspicillum)*, clown anemonefish (there are six species here), bumphead parrotfish *(Bolbometopon muricatum)*, pufferfish and porcupinefish that reside in the grottos along with morays and groupers. The shady areas gleam with small flashlightfish *(Photoblepharon palpebratus)* and teem with sweetlips, squirrelfish and whitetip reef sharks *(Triaenodon obesus)*, which in the open waters make way for grey sharks and barracuda, hundreds of which swim in the waters around Barracuda Point. Despite its favorable conditions, Sipadan is only one of the possible stops in this area. There are also numerous marine parks, which are not, however, always easily accessible and are not necessarily ideal locations for sport dives. Nevertheless, some of these protected sites provide opportunities to encounter impressive creatures like the whale shark. An unusual place to visit, which provides the opportunity to see a different environment, is the atoll of Layang Layang, which consists of a dozen emerging reefs lying above what could be an ancient extinct volcano or the slope of a submerged mountain, the base of which is nearly 2,000 meters deep. The atoll, more than seven kilometres long and little more than two kilometers wide, surrounds a deep lagoon about 60 meters deep. Its isolated position makes it an ideal place to see large pelagic species: carangids, barracuda, tunas, manta rays and hammerhead sharks, all making use of the violent currents that bring in large quantities of plankton, the first link in the particularly rich food chain. This has some consequences on the visibility of the water, which is not always perfectly clear in the upper levels. The lower levels, which require a good deal of experience to dive, are more sheltered and teem with marine fauna.

Here there are numerous large angelfish, such as *Pomacanthus xanthometopon*, lionfish (*Pterois* sp.), turkeyfish and the fearsome stonefish (*Synanceia* sp.), not to mention groupers and morays or eagle rays (*Aetobatus narinari*) which patrol the dense stretches of black corals.

From this unusual atoll our exploration of marine life in the eastern seas of Southeast Asia will take us to Borneo and Indonesia, areas perhaps even more rich, so much so that even a non-expert may easily encounter over 50 different, medium-sized species during a single dive. As is almost always the rule, life is particularly vigorous in the first 20 meters. Light, which is rarely a limiting factor, permits the development of algae and especially the zooxanthellae associated with corals, the growth of which helps create extremely complex habitats. In the areas closer to the surface, the tides, which fluctuate from one to three meters, regulate not only the position of the various species of coral, but the movements of the fish, many of which rise upwards and approach the reef when the high tide covers the corals, carrying in the mucus which covers them to keep them damp. For many species this mucus is a food source that is supplemented by plankton and detritus suspended in the currents. Anthias, wrasses, parrotfish, angelfish and butterflyfish live along the reef according to their habits. Some are territorial, while others, more dependent on food availability, swim from one point to another in search of food. This behavior is not only found in fish. Crown-of-thorns starfish *(Acanthaster planci)* can be frequent, and this may make it possible to observe how they feed on coral polyps, and how in their turn they are hunted by sea tritons *(Charonia tritonis)*, which pin them down with their foot and then divide them into pieces using their sturdy radula. Wherever one looks, the world appears brightly colored and peaceful, but this is only an illusion. In reality there is nothing more "ravenous" than a coral reef. Even the smallest, most insignificant organisms are intent on hunting and avoiding being eaten. The starfish that move by crawling along the seabed using their pedicels equipped with suckers are actually scraping and eating minuscule algae and microorganisms from the substratum. The lively plumes of the crinoids are nothing more than nets placed in the water to capture prey. The colorful sea slugs, often gathered in groups intent on mating, use their vivid colors to avoid being disturbed, while they themselves are relentless hunters of sponges, hydroids and corals. Reproduction is the other activity which seems to predominate on the reef. Often divers will see only its traces, such as the baskets of eggs of the Spanish dancer (*Hexabranchus sanguineus)* or the oviparous cords of a squid. If they are lucky, they may witness the courting ritual of the butterflyfish or parrotfish that swim in pairs toward the surface in order to deposit their eggs and spermatozoa, or they may see gobies fighting for the attentions of a female. These waters, which are still relatively unfrequented, give divers the opportunity to observe organisms and events never before witnessed, and which in fact may only be visible here. Having a spirit ready to accept what nature offers can make the difference between an exciting dive and a mediocre one. Always respect your surroundings. Although the forms of life on the reef may seem strange, remember that divers are the true foreigners. You have an abiding duty to make every effort to leave no trace of your passage.

GINGLYMOSTOMATIDAE FAMILY

Nurse shark
Nebrius ferrugineus

Body is tapered and flattened ventrally. Snout is characterized by a pair of lateral barbels. Prefers to remain on the seabed sheltered in grottos during the day. At night it is active, hunting fish and mollusks. Up to 3.2 meters in size.

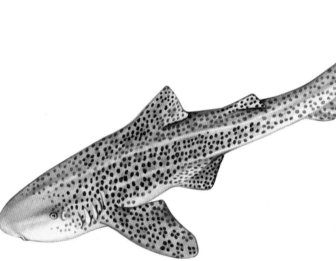

STEGOSTOMATIDAE FAMILY

Leopard shark
Stegostoma fasciatum

Body is elongated in the front and terminates with a long tail with only one upper lobe. Back is characterized by clear longitudinal protuberances extending to the second dorsal fin. Its belly is flattened. Adults are brownish-yellowish in color with numerous dark spots. Young individuals are blackish and streaked with white. A solitary species, during the day it prefers to remain immobile on the sandy bottom of the reef. It is more active at night, when it hunts mollusks and crustaceans. Can reach 3.5 meters in size.

CARCHARHINIDAE FAMILY

Grey reef shark
Carcharhinus amblyrhynchos

A rather common shark in the Maldives, where it is not rare to see at least two or three swimming along the walls that drop to the deeper seabeds. Easily recognizable by its somewhat stocky form and its color, which tends to be grey, with the white back edge of the first dorsal fin and the black edge of the tail standing out. Prefers to feed on fish, but does not disdain other reef animals. Reaches about two meters in length.

CARCHARHINIDAE FAMILY

Whitetip reef shark
Triaenodon obesus

Tips of the dorsal and caudal fins are white. Upper lobe of the caudal fin is elongated. Teeth are small. Eyes have a nictitating membrane. Reaches two meters in length. It is considered harmless and tends to stay away from humans, but it is best not to underestimate it and to consider it potentially dangerous. Appears to be territorial.

SPHYRNIDAE FAMILY

Scalloped hammerhead shark
Sphyrna lewini

Tapered, stocky body with large head with undulated front
edge. Tends to form schools when
young. Is not considered aggressive.
Feeds on fish, including other sharks
and rays, which it captures on the seabed by killing
them with violent blows of the head. Up to 4.2 meters
in size.

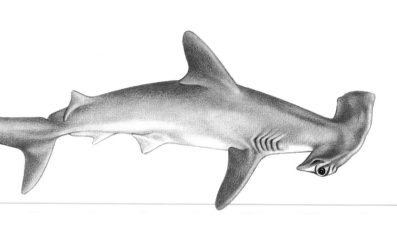

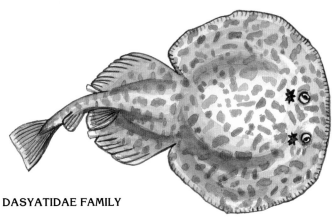

TORPEDINIDAE FAMILY

Marbled electric ray
Torpedo marmorata

Body shaped like a flattened disk, ventral fin on back that
terminates in a thick, sturdy tail, with two dorsal fins and a
well-developed caudal fin. Captures its prey by stunning it
with an electric shock that can even stun a man. Lives on the
sandy seabeds of the reef. Including the tail, up to 80
centimeters in diameter.

DASYATIDAE FAMILY

Blue-spotted ribbontail stingray
Taeniura lymma

Disk-shaped body is flattened and slightly elongated. Back is
yellowish brown with characteristic, unmistakable blue spots.
There are one to two sturdy poisonous spines on the tail.
Common in sandy areas among coral formations and often
seen below *Acropore* umbrellas or at the entry to grottos. Feeds
on crustaceans and mollusks. Including the tail, it measures up
to 2.40 meters in size.

Giant reef ray
Taeniura melanospilos

Rounded, clearly disk-shaped body with slightly upraised
edges. Its eyes are raised and immediately behind them are the
large spotholes that permit it to breathe even when it is
resting on the seabed. Its back is rough due to the
presence of tubercles. The tail, longer than the
diameter of the disk, has one or two poisonous
spines with serrated edges. Its back is greyish with
brownish or black spots which sometimes converge.
Its belly is light-colored. It can be found on sheltered
sandy seabeds or in grottos. Up to one meter in diameter.

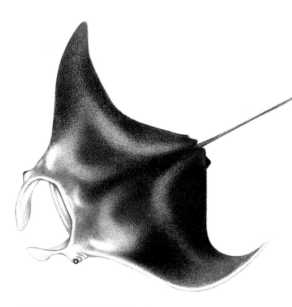

MOBULIDAE FAMILY
Manta ray
Manta birostris

Wide body and ventrally flattened back. Easily distinguished by the large cephalic fins located at the sides of its mouth. Pectoral fins are quite developed and permit the fish to reach five to six meters in width.

MYLIOBATIDAE FAMILY

Spotted eagle ray
Aetobatus narinari

Easily be identified by its pointed, bulging head with large eyes and broad lateral spotholes. Its lozenge-shaped body has broad pointed pectoral fins. Its tail, with one to three toothed spines, is about three times as long as the body. Ventral fins are enlarged and fleshy. Back is dark with many small white spots. Disk measures up to two meters wide. Can reach 2.5 meters in total length. Found in shallow lagoons (one to five meters in depth) on sandy seabeds.

MURAENIDAE FAMILY

Giant moray
Gymnothorax javanicus

Considered the largest of the morays and is quite common. Body is robust, rather wide at the trunk, and terminates in a well-developed head. Snout is short with a large mouth. The openings on the large black opercules are quite evident. Body is characterized by three rows of dark brown spots. Tail is reticulate. Can reach 2.5 meters in length.

Reticulated moray
Gymnothorax tessellata

Elongated and tapered, snake-like body. Snout is pointed and ends in a wide mouth armed with strong teeth. It is black with yellow streaks that form a very regular crisscross pattern. Lives in crevice-filled reef areas and near wrecks. Can be aggressive. Up to 1.5 meters long.

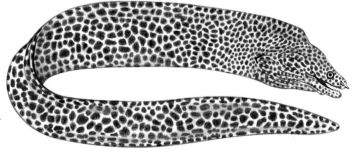

146

Peppered moray
Siderea picta

Rounded, massive snout and conical teeth arranged in two rows on its palate. Light-colored with tiny dark spots which take the form of small circles in young individuals. Lives on coastal seabeds and tidal areas. Has sometimes been observed following prey (crustaceans and fish) out of the water. Up to 1.20 meters in size.

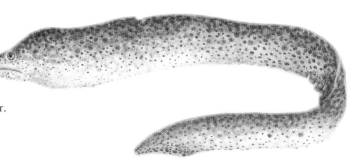

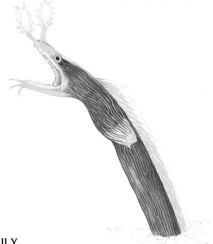

CONGRIDAE FAMILY

Black-spotted garden eel
Heteroconger hassi

This is a very elusive animal which immediately flees when approached by divers. It lives in large colonies in sandy areas, usually more than 20 meters in depth, and leaves the upper portion of the body protruding as it floats on the water in search of the plankton on which it feeds. The head has a short snout, with large eyes and an oblique mouth with large lips. The body is light-colored, dotted with numerous dark spots and some larger ones near the back. The species reaches 40 centimeters in length.

Ribbon eel
Rhynomuraena quaesita

A ribbon-shaped eel. Easily recognizable by its pointed snout and long jaws. Lower jaw has barbels; upper one has long, developed fringed nostrils. Young eels are blackish in color, males are blue with yellow fins, and females are all yellow. This species has a sexual inversion from male to female. Ribbon eels prefer sandy or detrital seabeds and generally leave only the front of their bodies exposed. Feeds on fish and crustaceans. Reaches 1.2 meters in length.

PLOTOSIDAE FAMILY

Striped catfish
Plotosus lineatus

Elongated fish with a second dorsal fin that extends to the tail, where it joins with the anal fin, also well-developed. Snout is characterized by four pairs of barbels. Sharp poisonous spines are located in front of the pectoral fins and on the first dorsal fin. It has white longitudinal stripes. Young catfish are gregarious, while adults are solitary. Feeds on small invertebrates. Can reach 32 centimeters long.

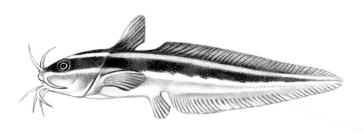

ANTENNARIDAE FAMILY

Sargassumfish
Histrio histrio

Founded, almost spherical body, with small fins. Body is covered with numerous irregular appendages similar to algae, which offer it perfect camouflage among the floating algae. It is a brownish green color with yellowish and variegated tones. Feeds on small invertebrates and fish. Up to 14 centimeters long.

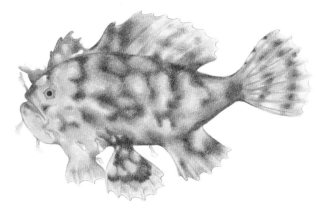

HOLOCENTRIDAE FAMILY
White-tipped soldierfish
Myripristis vittata

Sub-oval body with blunt snout and large eyes. Dorsal fin has sturdy, spiny, white-tipped rays which are the most distinctive feature of the species. Red-orange in color. Lives in groups in grottos and less illuminated areas of the reef. Up to 20 centimeters in size.

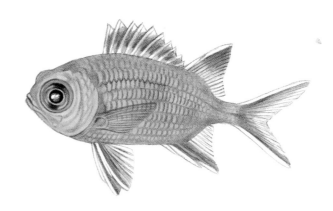

Saber squirrelfish
Sargocentron spiniferum

Wide, fairly compressed body. Pointed snout with relatively large eyes. Dorsal fin is well-developed with a red interradial membrane. Body is red with red spots which are darker on the operculum and at the base of the pectoral fins. A nocturnal species, it has an aggressive nature due to its territorial habits. Up to 45 centimeters long.

ANOMALOPIDAE FAMILY

Small flashlightfish
Photoblepharon palpebratus

Sturdy oval body that terminates in a long peduncle that supports a clearly forked tail. Its principal characteristic is the possession of luminous organs situated below the eyes that can be extinguished by strips of skin. On moonless nights it can be observed along the grotto-filled walls of the reef. Up to 12 centimeters in length.

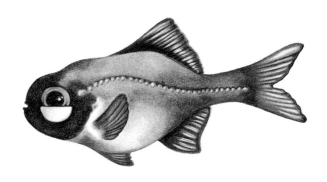

FISTULARIIDAE FAMILY

Trumpetfish
Fistularia commersoni

Cylindrical body that terminates in a long, tubular snout. Dorsal and anal fins are symmetrical and placed quite far back. Caudal fin has two central rays which are quite slender and elongated. Its color may vary due to its excellent mimetic abilities as it lies in wait to capture the small prey on which it feeds. It is not uncommon to see it swimming hidden by the body of larger, harmless fish, in order to approach its prey unobserved. Up to 1.5 meters in size.

SOLENOSTOMIDAE FAMILY

Ghost pipefish
Solenostomus cyanopterus

Elongated and compressed body covered with star-shaped dermal scales. Snout is long and trumpet-shaped, while its caudal peduncle is short and supports an oval-shaped tail. Ventral fins are well-developed and include the pocket in which the females incubate their eggs. It is a solid greenish or brownish color. Lives on shallow, algae-covered seabeds. Up to 16 centimeters in length.

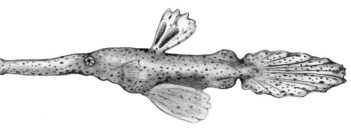

PEGASIDAE FAMILY

Short dragonfish
Euripegasus draconis

Body flattened dorso-ventrally and protected by a sturdy armor of bony plates. Snout is elongated and forms a sort of proboscis which the fish uses to suck up the small invertebrates on which it feeds. Ventral fins are quite large and broad and are used during locomotion. Lives on sandy seabeds in sheltered areas. It is light-colored with blue-edged fins. Up to seven centimeters in size.

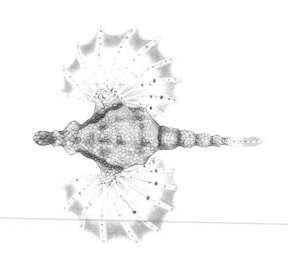

PLATYCEPHALIDAE FAMILY

Crocodile fish
Cociella crocodila

Body covered with rough scales. Flattened head with eyes in an almost dorsal position, with irregular lids. Mouth is large and armed with small pointed teeth. Remains immobile on the seabed lying in wait for prey. Up to 70 centimeters long.

SCORPAENIDAE FAMILY

Spiny devilfish
Inimicus didactylus

Robust, slightly compressed body with a slightly convex dorsal profile. Head is quite robust and has a clear concave area between the mouth and the eyes, which appear almost raised. Dorsal fin has spiny rays which are quite distinct from each other. The initial rays of the pectoral fins are separate. Its color, dark with yellowish ornamentation, is quite mimetic. Lives on sandy or muddy seabeds, where it often burrows. Up to 18 centimeters in length.

Zebra lionfish
Dendrochirus zebra

Robust, tapered body, wider in the central portion near the dorsal fin, which has spiny rays that are quite long and almost fully separated one from the other. Two long, irregular tentacles can be seen above the eyes. Its operculum is distinguished by a characteristic black spot. Lives on detrital seabeds with coral masses. Up to 18 centimeters in length.

Turkeyfish
Pterois volitans

Body similar to the zebra lionfish. Has large brown vertical stripes which are not all the same size. The rays of the fins are not bare, but have a more or less developed membrane which makes them similar to feathers. The uneven fins have rows of brown-black spots. Around the mouth and above the eyes are clear uneven appendages. Reaches 30-35 centimeters in length.

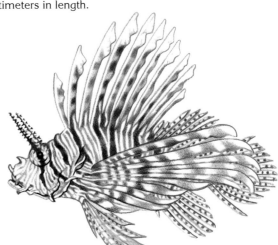

Tassled scorpionfish
Scorpaenopsis oxycephala

Robust body which is slightly compressed and raised in the middle. Head is massive with a large mouth surrounded by numerous growths which also extend around the eyes. The initial spines on the dorsal fin, which are poisonous, are all about the same size. It is extremely varied in color and quite mimetic. Lives along the outer edges of the reef on coral and detrital seabeds. Up to 36 centimeters in length.

Stonefish
Synanceia verrucosa

Massive, robust body with sunken head and almost vertical mouth. Practically invisible due to its color and the form of its body, it is one of the true dangers of the tropical seas. Its spines are extremely poisonous. Up to 35 centimeters in length.

Leaf scorpionfish
Taenionotus triacanthus

Body similar to a scorpionfish with a large head, oblique mouth and tapered and compressed body at the end. The upper portion of the eye is characterized by uneven appendages. Dorsal fin is well-developed, with poisonous spiny rays. Its coloring is quite varied and mimetic, which makes it possible to slowly approach the small fish on which it feeds, like a leaf carried on the current. Reaches 10-12 centimeters in length.

SERRANIDAE FAMILY

Flag basslet
Pseudanthias squamipinnis

Oval, compressed body that terminates in a falcate tail with elongated lobes. Snout is short and rounded with a terminal mouth. Dorsal fin is developed, especially in males, which have several quite long front rays. It is reddish in color with red spots near the pectoral fins. Females have yellowish tones. A gregarious fish which forms schools dominated by one or two males. Reaches 15-17 centimeters in length.

Purple anthias
Pseudanthias tuka

Fish with a tapered form with clearly falcate tail. Both sexes are purple, but males can be identified by the red spot at the base of the dorsal fin, which extends along the back, and the more developed upper lip. Females have a yellow streak on the back, and the edges of the caudal fins are yellow. Forms dense schools at the edges of the outer reef and in the channels of lagoons. Up to 12 centimeters in length.

Peach anthias
Pseudanthias dispar

Oval, compressed body with long dorsal and caudal fins which are clearly forked. Males can be distinguished by the red dorsal fin, yellowish background color and larger upper lip. Lives on the outer slope of reefs and near passes, where it gathers in large schools. Feeds on plankton. Up to 9.5 centimeters long.

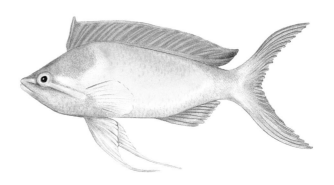

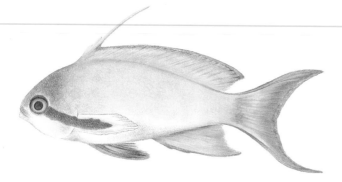

Red-cheeked anthias
Pseudanthias huchthii

Oval, compressed body with falcate tail. Males have a greenish background color with a red band that extends from the mouth to the operculum. Dorsal fin is edged in red. Males are territorial and form harems. Lives in lagoons near internal coral formations and along the passes up to a depth of 20 meters. Up to 13 centimeters in length.

Coral grouper
Cephalopholis miniata

Tapered, robust body, slightly compressed at the sides. A rather common species, it can be found especially along the channels that cross the reef and where the water is most limpid. Feeds primarily on fish. Up to 40 centimeters long.

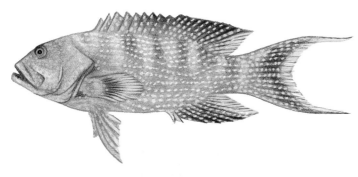

Lyretail grouper
Variola louti

Tapered body, easily recognizable both due to its bright color and the large sickle-shaped caudal fin, which is often edged with yellow. Appears most frequently around coral islands. Up to 80 centimeters long.

GRAMMISTIDAE FAMILY

Six-stripe soapfish
Grammistes sexlineatus

Robust, oval body slightly compressed at the sides. A timid species, it tends to remain in grottos and crevices. If threatened, its skin can produce a mucous which is toxic to other fish. Up to 30 centimeters in length.

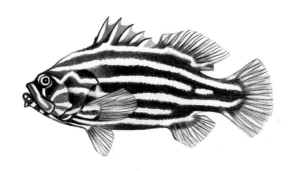

PLESIOPIDAE FAMILY

Comet
Calloplesiops altivelis

Elongated body, with a wide mouth and large eyes. Dorsal and anal fins are quite developed and appear almost joined to the very broad and rounded caudal fin. It is blackish in color with numerous small light spots. The large black spot edged in white at the end of the dorsal fin is typical of the species. When it takes refuge in a crevice it leaves its tail out, and the spot mimics the head of a large moray. Up to 16 centimeters long.

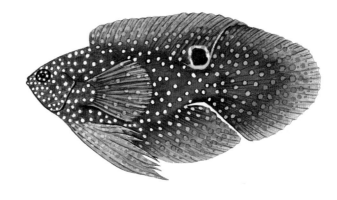

CIRRHITHIDAE FAMILY

Pixy hawkfish
Cirrhitichthys oxycephalus

Elongated, slender body with slightly pointed snout. Dorsal fin has hairy tufts at the tip of spiny rays. Sedentary in habit, it can often be observed immobile on corals, where it may move in rapid jerks. The larger males are territorial. Up to 9-10 centimeters in length.

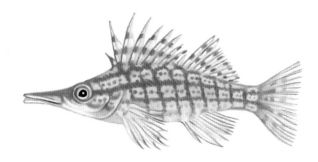

APOGONIDAE FAMILY

Ring-tailed cardinalfish
Apogon aureus

Fusiform body, large eyes, wide mouth and two dorsal fins. It is golden in color. Around the eyes are light blue stripes and the caudal peduncle is black. Favours the less illuminated parts of the reef such as caves and crevices, emerging from these in small shoals to feed on plankton. Up to 12 centimetres long.

PSEUDOCHROMIDAE FAMILY

Royal dottyback
Pseudochromis paccagnellae

The species' curious Latin name comes from the name of the man who discovered it, the Italian Werner Paccagnella. Tapered body can be recognized by its bright, dual coloring: the front part is violet and the back is yellow. More common along the outside slopes of the reef and in the channels of lagoons. Up to seven centimeters long.

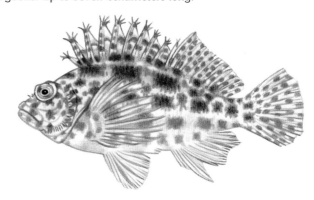

Longnose hawkfish
Oxicirrhites typus

The body is slightly tapered and terminates with an elongated snout. The dorsal fin has frilled tips on each spine. The background color is whitish with a series of red stripes that form a checkerboard on its body mimetic with gorgonians. Lives usually at more than 20 meters of depth along the outer reefs. Up to thirteen centimeters long.

152

PRIACANTHIDAE FAMILY

Goggle-eye
Priacanthus hamrur

Oval, wide and compressed body. Short snout with large eyes. Mouth is tilted upwards. It is generally a dark reddish color, but can change rapidly, acquiring silvery reflections and red streaks. Dorsal and anal fins are tinged dark along the edges. During the day it stays within grottos, and it comes out at night to hunt. Reaches 40-45 centimeters long.

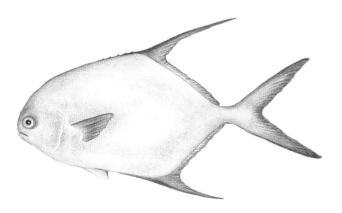

ECHENEIDAE FAMILY

Sharksucker
Echeneis naucrates

Elongated body flattened at the back. It is typically associated with larger fish such as sharks and mantas, to which it adheres using the sucker created from the dorsal fin. Feeds on the parasites of the fish to which it attaches itself, but can swim and hunt independently. Up to 1.1 meters in length.

CARANGIDAE FAMILY

Bigeye Trevally
Caranx sexfasciatus

Elongated and compressed body with a rounded dorsal profile. Lower jaw protrudes. There are quite evident ridges on the caudal peduncle. Back is bluish-gray or bluish-green in color. The lobes of the caudal fin are blackish, and the tip of the second dorsal fin is often white. Lives in schools along the reef and hunts at night. Measures up to 90 centimeters long.

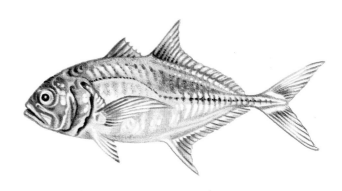

Silver pompano
Trachinotus blochii

Oval, tapered and compressed body with inclined upper snout. Dorsal and anal fins are symmetrical and opposite. Caudal fin is clearly forked with thin, elongated lobes. It is silvery-colored with spots on its sides and has yellowish fins. Young individuals live in sandy coastal areas and along estuaries. Adults prefer the outer reef areas. Up to 1.1 meters long.

Rainbow runner
Elagatis bipinnulata

Elongated and spindle-shaped with a pointed head and snout and a small mouth with numerous pointed teeth. Behind the dorsal and anal fins are two small opposite fins. Back is an olive blue color, with a light-colored stomach. Flanks are yellow with two light blue longitudinal streaks. Lives in schools along reefs. Up to 1.2 meters long.

LUTJANIDAE FAMILY

Two-spot red snapper
Lutjanus bohar

Massive, rather wide and rounded body. Large eyes and mouth with pointed canine teeth. The pre-operculum has a slight incisure. Pectoral fins are edged in black. Back is a reddish-bronze color, with a lighter-colored stomach. There are two distinct pearly spots on the dorsal fin. Lives in the deeper areas of the reef. Up to 75 centimeters in length.

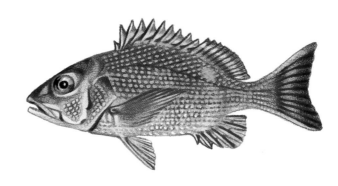

Bluelined snapper
Lutjanus kasmira

Tapered, compressed body with pointed snout and forked tail. Identified by the longitudinal blue stripes on its sides. May form schools of up to 1,000 individuals which gather around isolated coral pinnacles or wrecks. Is nocturnal, and by day stays sheltered among the corals. Up to 35 centimeters in length.

Mangrove snapper
Lutjanus argentimaculatus

Tapered and compressed but robust body. Snout is pointed and it has a large mouth with pointed canine teeth. A primarily coastal species, when young it can frequently be observed at the mouths of rivers. By day it tends to gather in groups. Feeds on crustaceans, cephalopods and fish. Up to 1.2 meters long.

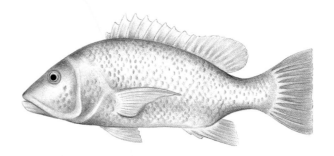

CAESIONIDAE FAMILY

Yellowback fusilier
Caesio teres

Tapered, cylindrical body which terminates in a clearly forked caudal fin with pointed lobes. Mouth is slightly turned upward, with a strongly protruding upper jaw suitable for gathering plankton. It is bluish in color with an upper yellow band that extends from the base of the dorsal fin to the caudal fin. Lives in schools in open water along the reef. Up to 31 centimeters in length.

Yellowtop fusilier
Caesio xanthonota

Tapered, cylindrical body that terminates with a clearly forked caudal fin with pointed lobes. Mouth is tilted slightly upward, with a strongly protruding upper jaw suitable for gathering plankton. It is bluish in color with an upper yellow band which extends from the dorsal fin to the caudal fin. Lives in large schools along the reef and in deeper lagoons. Up to 30 centimeters long.

HAEMULIDAE FAMILY

Lined sweetlips
Pletorhynchus lineatus

Robust body, compressed at the sides. Its head is rounded and convex. Its mouth is sub-terminal with large lips and small conical teeth. Its tail is slightly sunken. It is either solitary or lives in groups at the base of corals where there is little illumination. At night it hunts crustaceans on the sandy seabeds. Up to 72 centimeters in size.

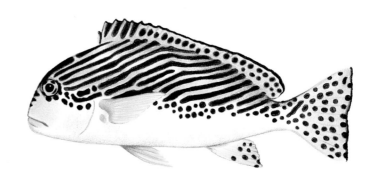

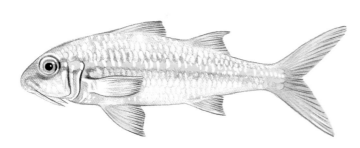

Spotted sweetlips
Plectorhynchus picus

Robust body, compressed at the sides. Head is rounded and convex. Mouth is sub-terminal with large lips and small conical teeth. Tail is slightly sunken. Young individuals are white with wide black bands that flow into each other. Adults have numerous dark spots. Is solitary and lives at the base of corals or in grottos, at depths of up to 50 meters. Feeds on crustaceans. Up to 84 centimeters long.

LETHRINIDAE FAMILY

Bigeye emperor
Monotaxis grandoculis

Robust, wide body flattened at the sides. Snout is blunt and terminates in a mouth with thick lips, canine teeth in front and molar-type teeth in the back of the jaw. Has large eyes. It is silvery with brownish tones. Prefers sandy seabeds up to 100 meters deep. Is nocturnal. Up to 60 centimeters in length.

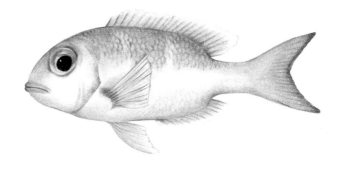

MULLIDAE FAMILY

Yellowfin Goatfish
Mulloidichthys vanicolensis

Elongated body which is nearly flat in the ventral area and wider in front. Mouth is small, and below the chin are the characteristic barbels typical of the family. Has a lateral yellow stripe extending from the eye to the tail. Fins are yellow. By day this species forms dense schools which stay near sandy seabeds. By night it is an active hunter. Up to 38 centimeters in length.

PEMPHERIDAE Family

Pigmy sweeper
Parapriacanthus ransonneti

Compressed, oval body with elongated caudal peduncle and convex snout. Mouth is small and tilted upward. Eyes are well-developed. Lives in dense schools in grottos or under large colonies of hard corals. At night they separate to hunt plankton. Up to 10 centimeters in length.

KIPHOSIDAE FAMILY

Highfin rudderfish
Kiphosus cinerascens

Body tends to be oval and compressed at the flanks. Snout is blunt with a small terminal mouth armed with incisors. Prefers sandy areas rich in vegetation near the line of shallows. By day lives in groups, which separate at night. Up to 45 centimeters in length.

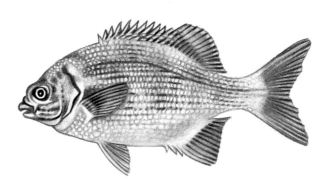

EPHIPPIDAE FAMILY

Longfin spadefish
Platax teira

Body is compressed and wide, almost disk-shaped, with well-developed dorsal and anal fins. Small terminal mouth has teeth similar to brushes, which it uses to scrape algae and small invertebrates from the seabed. Identified in particular by the black spot in front of the anal fin. Frequently found in lagoons. Adults live in pairs. Up to 60 centimeters long.

CHAETODONTIDAE FAMILY

Threadfin butterflyfish
Chaetodon auriga

Sub-rectangular body is quite wide and compressed. Head is concave in front and terminates in a short, pointed snout. A large dark band covers its eyes and narrows out along the back. Back part of the dorsal fin has a dark ocellate spot surmounted by several elongated, thready rays which are one of the characteristics traits of this species. *Chaetodon auriga* is solitary or lives in pairs. Measures 20-25 centimeters in length

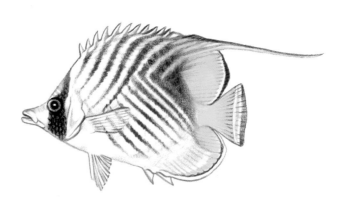

Triangle butterflyfish
Chaetodon baronessa

Wide, compressed body with pointed mouth and concave profile at the back of the head. Body tends to be dark with light angled streaks and orange bands at the edges of the fins. Lives in lagoons and along the reef, always remaining near colonies of Acropore coral, on the polyps of which it feeds exclusively. Up to 15 centimeters long.

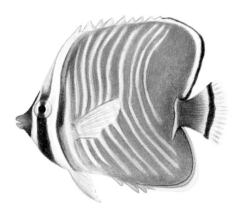

Ornate butterflyfish
Chaetodon ornatissimus

Oval, compressed body with pointed snout. Dorsal and anal fins are symmetrical and extend backward to reach the caudal fin, which has a rounded edge. Adults live in pairs and are territorial, preferring areas rich in corals alternating with broad open areas. Feeds on coral polyps. Up to 20 centimeters in length.

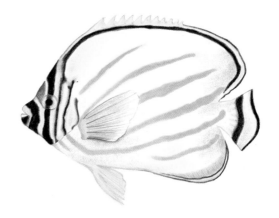

Meyer's butterflyfish
Chaetodon meyeri

Oval, compressed body with pointed snout. The dorsal and anal fins are symmetrical and extend backward to the caudal fin, which has a rounded edge. It has black horizontal stripes which tend to converge on the back. Adults are territorial and live in pairs. Feeds on coral polyps. Up to 18 centimeters in size.

Forcepsfish
Forcipiger flavissimus

Compressed body which ends in a long snout. Dorsal fin has well-developed, separate rays. Ventral fins are thready and extend beyond the base of the anal fin. It is almost entirely yellow in color, with the exception of a black spot at the base of the tail and the snout, the upper portion of which is dark with a whitish lower portion. Due to its long snout, this species is specialized in feeding on the protruding appendages of benthonic invertebrates. Up to 22 centimeters long.

POMACANTHIDAE FAMILY

Bicolor angelfish
Centropyge bicolor

Oval, compressed body characterized by its two colors. Front portion is entirely yellow, with the exception of a blue spot above the eyes, while the back portion is blue with the sole exception of the yellow caudal fin. Prefers coralline seabeds and sheltered areas such as lagoons, but never ventures far from its refuges. Up to 15 centimeters long.

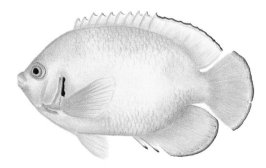

Lemonpeel angelfish
Centropyge flavissimus

Oval, compressed body. Mouth is small and armed with slender teeth similar to tweezers. Lives in harems composed of one male and several females. Prefers areas rich in corals, both in lagoons and along the outer reef to a depth of 25 meters. Feeds on algae. Up to 14 centimeters long.

Blue-ringed angelfish
Pomacanthus annularis

Angelfish with a wide, compressed body. Dorsal fin has elongated back rays. Anal fin has a rounded edge. Its coloration is characteristic due to the blue diagonal bands on its flanks which tend to join at the end of the dorsal fin. Young individuals are bluish-black with narrow white and blue vertical stripes. Is mostly solitary or lives in pairs, and is not uncommon in bays and sheltered areas with murky waters. Feeds on sponges and algae. Can reach 45 centimeters long.

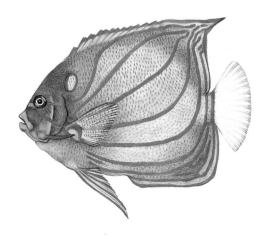

Semicircle angelfish
Pomacanthus semicirculatus

Wide, compressed body in a sub-rectangular form. Back of the head is concave. Mouth is terminal and armed with small slender teeth. Dorsal and anal fins extend backward with slender rays that reach the height of the caudal fin. Prefers areas rich in corals and frequents grottos and wrecks. Up to 38 centimeters long.

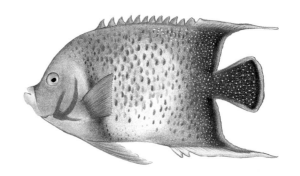

Blue-girdled fish
Pomacanthus navarchus

Wide, compressed body with short snout and small mouth. Its coloring is characteristic. Front, ventral and back portions are blue and are clearly separated by a wide orange-yellow area dotted with small blue spots. Throat and the dorsal and caudal fins are yellow. When young, up to eight centimeters in size, it is black with seven to eight vertical blue stripes on the flanks. Common along more sheltered coastal reefs and in lagoons. Up to 30 centimeters long.

POMACENTRIDAE FAMILY
Black anemonefish
Amphiprion melanopus

Body oval and stout, slightly compressed. Lives in sholas in lagoons and reef to 15-20 meters, more often commensal with the anemone *Entacmaea quadricolor*. The body is blackish and red-orange. There is a single white bar behind the eye. Pelvic and anal fins are black. Up to 12 centimeters long.

Clark's anemonefish
Amphiprion clarki

Small, oval but robust body. Its color may vary greatly, but it always has two white vertical bands and a light-colored snout. Can be seen in association with a large number of sea anemone species, to a depth of 55 meters. Up to 13 centimeters long.

False clown anemonefish
Amphiprion ocellaris

Small, oval but robust body. It is orange yellow with three wide white bands edged in black, as are the fins. Lives in shallow, even murky water, in lagoons and along the reef. It is associated with at least three species of anemone, including *Heteractis magnifica*. Up to 11 centimeters long.

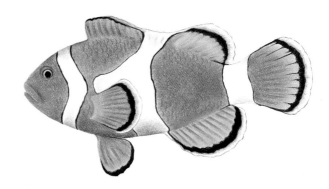

Orange anemonefish
Amphiprion sandaracinos

Small, oval but robust body. It is yellow with a white stripe in the center of the back of the head and at the base of the dorsal fin. Lives associated with anemones, in particular *Stichodactyla mertensii*. Lives in lagoons and along outer reefs up to about 20 meters deep. Feeds on algae and zooplankton. Up to 12 centimeters long.

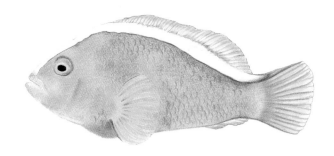

Spinecheek anemonefish
Premnas biaculeatus

Oval, slightly compressed body with small head and very short snout. Dorsal fin has a slight notch between the spiny rays and the soft ones. There is a large spine under the eye.
Males are bright red with three white equidistant bands. Females are less vivid in color and are sometimes almost black. In general it lives associated with the anemone *Entacmaea quadricolor*. Males are five to eight centimeters in size, while females may be two to three times as large.

Indo-Pacific sergeant
Abdudefduf vaigensis

Oval body with convex snout and small terminal mouth with conical teeth and incisors. Frequents a large variety of habitats: lagoons, flat seabeds and the slopes of reefs. Lives in schools and feeds on zooplankton, small invertebrates and seabed algae. Up to 20 centimeters long.

Blue devil
Chrysiptera cyanea

Oval body. Dorsal fin with distinct spiny rays. Caudal fin with rounded edge. Its color varies depending on sex. Males are blue with yellow tails, while females are all blue with a black spot on the back of the dorsal fin. Both sexes have a black streak that crosses the snout and the eye. Prefers lagoons and sheltered reefs. Up to eight centimeters in length.

Banded dascyllus
Dascyllus aruanus

Rather stocky, square body which is wide and compressed. Mouth is small, with a slightly protruding lower jaw. Its basic color is whitish, with three evident dark bands running transversally, the first of which covers the eyes and mouth. It forms small groups which are strictly associated with a single colony of hard corals. Only the largest individuals venture any distance from the corals, while the smaller ones remain permanently among the coral branches. Up to 8 to ten centimeters in size.

Bluntsnout gregory
Stegastes lividus

Small, oval body slightly compressed at the sides. Tail is forked. Snout is convex. Lives around colonies of hard corals and gathers in colonies in which individuals react quite aggressively to other species. Feeds on algae, which it defends from other herbivorous fish. If disturbed will emit deep sounds. Up to 13 centimeters long.

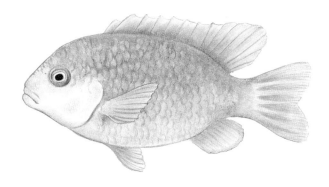

LABRIDAE FAMILY

Bluestreak cleaner wrasse
Labroides dimidiatus

Elongated and tapered body, compressed at the sides. Snout is pointed with a terminal mouth. This characteristic makes it possible to distinguish this species from the blennies that imitate it. It has blue and black stripes. It is the most typical of the cleaner wrasses and can always be seen near other fish, even large predators, as it cleans them of parasites. Up to 11 centimeters long.

Redbreasted maori wrasse
Cheilinus fasciatus

Compressed, stocky body wider in the front. Massive head with blunt profile. Mouth with thick lips and well-developed front teeth. Front portion behind the head to the ventral fins is scarlet red. Flanks are distinguished by six or seven dark bands, some of which extend to the dorsal fin, which has red spots, like the caudal and anal fins. Feeds on benthonic invertebrates. Up to 36 centimeters long.

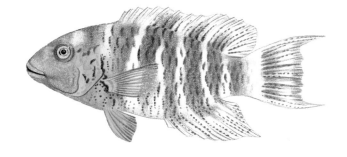

Slingjaw wrasse
Epibulus insidiator

Wide, robust body. Large head and mouth characterized by protruding jaws capable of transforming into a sort of large tube when they are completely extended. Females are totally yellow. Males have a white head. In both sexes a black streak crosses the eyes. An active predator, it feeds on fish and crustaceans. Up to 35 centimeters long.

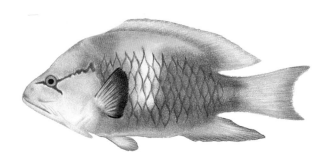

Yellowtail coris
Coris gaimard

Tapered, slender body with a form similar to the Mediterranean damselfish. The first two rays of the dorsal fin are typically elongated in adult males. The color is dusty with blue spots in the back and pale in the forehead. The head is tapered with green bands. The caudal fin is yellow. Juveniles are red with black-edged white saddles. Reaches 35-40 centimeters long.

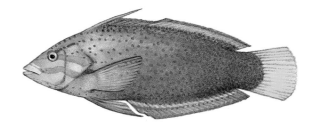

Moon wrasse
Thalassoma lunare

Spindle-shaped, sturdy body, slightly compressed. Rounded head and short snout. Small mouth with thin lips. Caudal fin is truncated in young individuals and crescent-shaped in adults, especially in the larger males, which are also bluish in color. It is greenish in color with purple-red vertical stripes on the flanks. Head is bluish-green with wide pinkish stripes which are nearly longitudinal. Caudal fin is yellowish in the center, with pinkish streaks along the lobes. Up to 25-30 centimeters long.

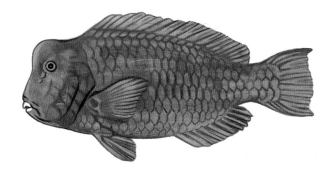

Bird wrasse
Gomphosus varius

Wrasse which is nearly unmistakable due to its tapered form, accentuated by the long snout that terminates in a small, protractile mouth. Adult males are a deep blue-green, while females have dark spots on their scales. Feeds primarily on crustaceans which it finds among the corals on the seabed. Prefers coral-rich lagoons and the outer reef to a depth of 30 meters. Up to 28 centimeters long.

SCARIDAE FAMILY

Bumphead parrotfish
Bolbometopon muricatum

Parrotfish with wide, compressed body, unmistakable due to the clearly visible protuberance on the back of the head and an almost vertical front profile of the snout. Mouth is partially turned downward. It is generally a brownish color, and young individuals are characterized by five vertical lines of small white dots on their flanks. Lives in groups to a depth of 30 meters, and feeds on corals and encrusted algae. Up to 1.2 meters long.

Bullethead parrotfish
Scarus sordidus

Body is generally the typical shape of parrotfish. The dental plates are clearly visible. Young individuals have horizontal stripes. As they grow, they become brown in color. Adult males are green with salmon-tipped scales. Cheeks are a bright orange which shades into yellow on the opercula. Oddly, this fish has green teeth, while females have a red mouth. Up to 40-50 centimeters long.

Bicolor Parrotfish
Cetoscarus bicolor

Body tends to be tapered and oval. Pointed snout. Caudal fin is sickle-shaped with pointed lobes. Females are brown with numerous dark spots on the lower part of the body. Males have a bluish head finely spattered with fuchsia. Back and flanks are green with the edges of the scales tipped in fuchsia. Lives in pairs. Up to 80 centimeters long.

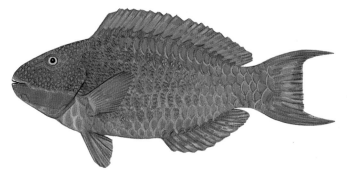

Pelenose parrotfish
Scarus psittacus

Tapered, oval body with oval head and terminal mouth.
Caudal fin is slightly sunken, with pointed lobes. Lives on flat
seabeds and in lagoons and along the outside slope of the reef,
to a depth of 25 meters. Often mixes with other species of
parrotfish in order to feed on coral polyps and algae.
At night it takes refuge in crevices and secretes a thick cocoon
of mucous. Up to 30 centimeters long.

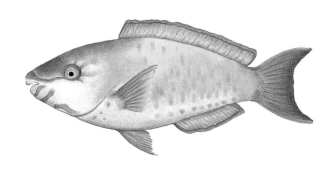

SPHYRAENIDAE FAMILY

Great barracuda
Sphyraena barracuda

Elongated, sub-cylindrical body with robust pointed head.
Mouth is large and armed with strong canine-type teeth. Lives
in schools when young, while adults gradually become solitary.
Lives in a great variety of habitats along the coast and in the
open sea. Feeds primarily on fish. Up to 1.9 meters in size.

SCOMBRIDAE FAMILY

Albacore
Thunnus alalunga

Tapered, powerful, extremely hydrodynamic body. Pointed
snout with terminal mouth. Caudal peduncle has a medial
longitudinal carina on each side. Pectoral fins are quite long
and reach the back edge of the dorsal fin. Back is dark blue
with silvery sides. Lives in the open sea and often ventures near
the coast. Feeds on fish. Up to 110 centimeters long.

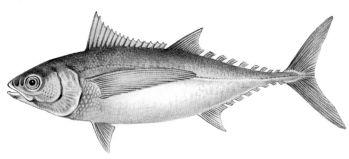

BLENNIDAE FAMILY

Striped fangblenny
Plagiotremus rhinorhynchus

Quite tapered body compressed on the sides. Snout is pointed
and the mouth is located below it. Dorsal fin extends along a
large part of the back. Caudal fin is preceded by a large
peduncle. Its black and blue stripes are quite similar to cleaner
fish, and in fact young *Plagiotremus* imitate them quite well.
Their mimetic coloring is used to attack other fish.
Up to 12 centimeters long.

MICRODESMIDAE FAMILY

Firefish
Nemateleotris magnifica

Elongated body, rounded in the front with back portion
compressed. Short snout with large eyes. Wide mouth with
large canine teeth. Has two dorsal fins, the first of which has
front rays which are quite long and erect, while the second is
opposite to and symmetrical with the anal fin. It is light in color,
with yellow tones in the front portion, and red with black-
striped fins in the back portion. A territorial species that lives
in pairs in dens dug in the sand, where it takes refuge
approaching danger. Up to eight centimeters long.

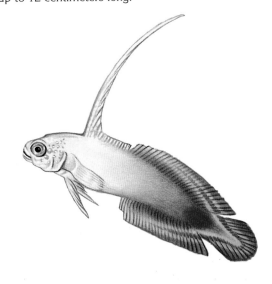

GOBIIDAE FAMILY

Gorgeous prawn-goby
Amblyeleotris wheeleri

Elongated body which terminates in a stubby, blunt head. Mouth is large with conical teeth. It has a double dorsal fin, with the front portion more developed. Ventral fins form a sort of adhesive disk. It is whitish in color with reddish vertical stripes. Males guard the eggs deposited by the females. Lives in lagoons and along the outer reefs to a depth of 15 meters. Up to eight centimeters long.

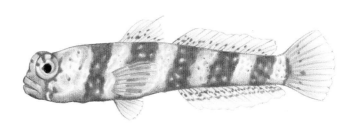

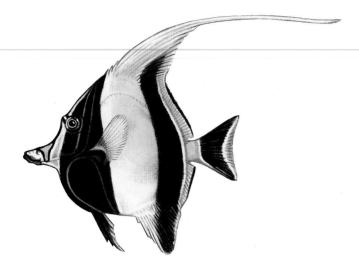

ZANCLIDAE FAMILY

Moorish idol
Zanclus cornutus

Wide, compressed body with concave head and elongated snout. Mouth is small and terminal. Dorsal fin has several quite elongated, sickle-shaped rays which extend beyond the caudal fin. Lives in quite varied environments, including bays of ports, lagoons and reefs, to a depth of 18 meters. Tends to gather in groups, which may vary in density. Feeds on sponges. Up to 16 centimeters long.

ACANTHURIDAE FAMILY

Spotted unicornfish
Naso brevirostris

The most characteristic of the surgeonfish, easily recognizable by its robust oval body that ends in a long beak that extends well past the snout. There are two bony plates at the sides of the peduncle, each with a sharp spine. Caudal fin is rounded. Its color varies from bluish gray to olive brown. Lips are sometimes bluish in color. Tail has a light band along the back edge. Gregarious. Up to 50 centimeters long.

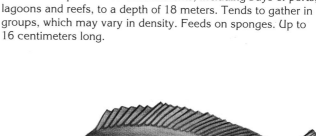

Blue-lined surgeonfish
Acanthurus lineatus

Elongated, oval and compressed body. Rounded snout. Sickle-shaped pectoral fins. Crescent-shaped caudal fin with very elongated lobes. Caudal peduncle with large spine. Flanks characterized by eight to 10 yellow and blue longitudinal stripes. Light-colored belly. Ventral fins are yellow with a black front edge. Territorial and aggressive, it is most common on reefs exposed to waves. Up to 38 centimeters in length.

Blue surgeonfish
Acanthurus leucosternon

Wide, oval and compressed body. Dorsal and anal fins are almost symmetrical and equally developed. Caudal fin is slightly sunken. White throat. Lives in groups of about 30 individuals, primarily in calm coastal waters. Feeds primarily on algae. Up to 23 centimeters long.

Brushtail tang
Zebrasoma scopas

Surgeonfish with the typical, almost disk-shaped form of the genus *Zebrasoma*. Dorsal and anal fins are quite developed. Snout is pointed. It is brownish in color, with narrow bluish streaks. The pointed spines on the caudal fin are white. Feeds on algae. It is more frequent in coral-rich lagoons and along the outer reef to a depth of 60 meters. Up to 20 centimeters long.

Bignose unicornfish
Naso vlammingi

Robust, tapered body which tends to be oval, with a snout with an almost vertical front profile. The caudal fin has quite elongated and thread-like lobes. During the day it tends to form schools which gather in the column of water above the reef. It feeds on plankton. Can change color rapidly.
Up to 70 centimeters in size.

Orangespine unicornfish
Naso lituratus

Oval body which is compressed and wide in front. Robust head with dorsal profile that forms about a 45° angle. Pointed snout, small mouth with incisors with rounded tips. There are two bony plates on the sides of the peduncle, each with a sharp, curved spine pointed out. Caudal fin is crescent-shaped with pointed lobes and long, thready rays. It is yellowish-brown in color. Caudal peduncle is orange. There is a light yellow spot between the eyes. Dorsal fin is yellow-orange, black at the base and white-edged. Reaches 45 centimeters in size.

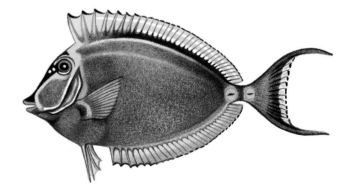

SIGANIDAE FAMILY

Foxface rabbitfish
Siganus vulpinus

Tapered, compressed body with small terminal mouth armed with incisor-type teeth. The spiny rays of its fins are poisonous and can cause painful wounds. The young of the species are gregarious, while adults live in pairs. Feeds on algae. Prefers areas rich in corals, in lagoons and along the outer reefs. Up to 24 centimeters long.

BOTHIDAE FAMILY

Peacock flounder
Bothus mancus

Oval body, flattened and almost disk-shaped, with both eyes on the left side. It is brownish grey, with large light blue ocelli. Males are distinguished by the very long rays of the pectoral fin. Lives on sandy seabeds in lagoons and along the reef, up to a depth of about 80 meters. Up to 42 centimeters long.

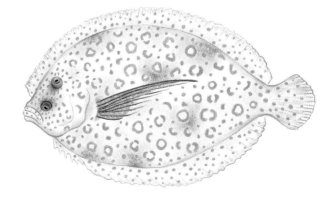

BALISTIDAE FAMILY

Yellow-margin triggerfish
Pseudobalistes flavimarginatus

The body form is that tipical of the family. Teeth are white, in two upper rows and only one lower row. Its background color is rather light. Front portion between the snout and the base of the pectoral fins is light yellow. Flanks have black spots. Edges of the dorsal, anal and caudal fins are yellowish. Up to 60 centimeters long.

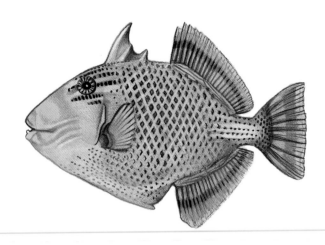

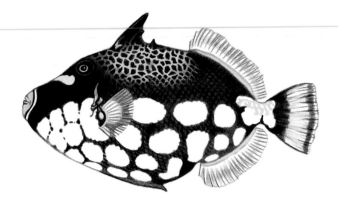

Clown triggerfish
Balistoides conspicillum

Wide, compressed body which tends to be oval. It is uncommon and is probably the most striking of the triggerfish species. It is solitary and prefers the steeper slopes of the reef with numerous grottos, to a depth of 70-75 meters. Up to 50 centimeters in size.

Redtooth triggerfish
Odonus niger

Sub-oval body. Pointed head. Terminal mouth with a more developed lower jaw. Teeth are canine and, curiously, red in color. Body is bluish-black, while the head is greenish with bluish stripes that start from the mouth. Caudal fin is crescent-shaped, with quite long and developed lobes. Tends to gather in small groups. Up to 50 centimeters long.

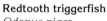

Picasso triggerfish
Rhinecanthus aculeatus

Sub-rhomboidal-shaped body with flattened sides. Lives in shallow waters (one to five meters in depth) in lagoons and flat reefs with sandy and detrital seabeds. Feeds on invertebrates and small fish. Up to 25 centimeters long.

MONACANTHIDAE FAMILY

Unicorn filefish
Aluteros monoceros

Very compressed, irregularly oval and elongated body. Snout is pointed and terminates in a small, rounded mouth. Second dorsal fin is preceded by another dorsal fin located above the eyes and reduced to two single spines, the first of which is quite developed. It is generally grey in color with small spots, but may change color to camouflage itself among the floating detritus where it often takes refuge. In general it is solitary and eats a great variety of food, from algae to plankton. Up to 75 centimeters long.

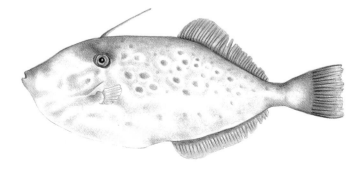

Scribbled filefish
Aluterus scriptus

Very compressed, irregularly oval and elongated body. Snout is pointed and terminates in a small rounded mouth. Second dorsal fin is preceded by another dorsal fin located above the eyes and reduced to two single spines, the first of which is quite developed. It is yellowish in color with bluish spots and streaks. In general solitary, it feeds on algae and invertebrates. Up to 1.1 meters in size.

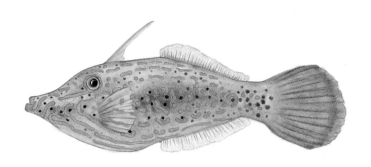

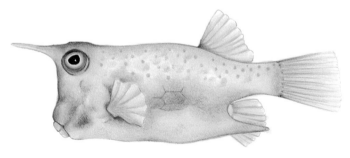

Longnose filefish
Oxymonacantus longirostris

Rounded, oval body that terminates in an elongated snout with a small mouth opening at the end. A long spine that corresponds to the first dorsal fin is located on the back above the eye. Second dorsal fin and the anal fin are similar and symmetrical. Lives in lagoons and along the outer reefs, feeding on *Acropore* coral polyps. Measures up to 12 centimeters long.

OSTRACIIDAE FAMILY

Cube boxfish
Ostracion cubicus

Box-shaped and rectangular, with rounded angles and corners and no spines. Dorsal and anal fins are small but have powerful muscles that propel the fish. Ventral and caudal fins are more developed and act as rudders. Males are brilliant yellow with blue backs. Females are a uniform violet color. Young individuals are yellow with black spots. Reaches 45 centimeters in length.

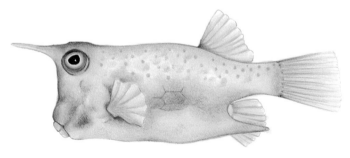

Longhorn cowfish
Lactoria cornuta

Polygonal body similar to a large rigid box composed of bony plates welded together. Eyes are in a dorsal position and are protected by two large spiny appendages. Mouth is small, with strong teeth suitable for crushing the small invertebrates it captures after removing the sediments that cover them. It is solitary and lives on sandy and detrital seabeds. Up to 46 centimeters long.

TETRAODONTIDAE FAMILY

Black-saddled toby
Canthigaster valentini

Elongated, rounded body covered with a thick skin but no scales. Mouth is small and has teeth fused together to form a sort of beak. If frightened, it swells up. It is territorial and lives in harems, and males mate with numerous females. Prefers mixed seabeds. It is imitated by *Paraluteres prionurus*. Feeds on algae and invertebrates. Up to 10 centimeters long.

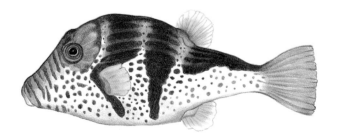

Black-spotted pufferfish
Arothron stellatus

Elongated, globular body with an oval profile, covered with small spines. In young individuals this is rubbery, while it is more limp in adults. Mouth is robust and armed with two large contiguous dental plates on each jaw. Its color is typically spotted. In young individuals the belly has evident black stripes. Base of the pectoral fins is black. Swims by propelling itself with the dorsal and anal fins. This species is not uncommon on the sandy bottoms of lagoons. Up to 90 centimeters long.

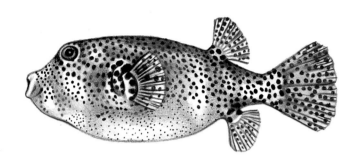

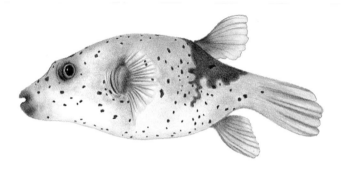

Black-spotted puffer
Arothron nigropunctatus

Large cylindrical body which terminates in a well-developed caudal peduncle which supports a rounded caudal fin. Snout is stubby with two pairs of nostrils. Its sturdy beak has a medial suture. Can be identified by its light color with small spots and dark-edged lips. Feeds on corals, sponges, ascidia and algae. Up to 30 centimeters long.

Map puffer
Arothron mappa

Globular but elongated body that terminates in a blunt snout on which two pairs of nostrils can be seen. Eyes are surrounded by a dense series of radial streaks. Is solitary and lives near refuges in lagoons and along sheltered reefs. Feeds on algae, sponges and other invertebrates. Up to 65 centimeters long.

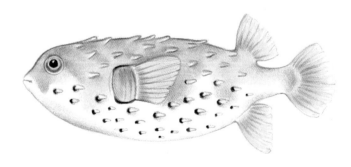

DIODONTIDAE FAMILY
Yellow-spotted burrfish
Ciclichthys spilostylus

Elongated and oval body similar to a rugby ball. Snout is short and blunt with large eyes. Its large dental plates form a sturdy beak suitable for cracking the shells of the mollusks and crustaceans on which it feeds. Body is covered with spines which bristle when the animal swells up by swallowing water. Nocturnal. Up to 34 centimeters long.

Black blotched porcupinefish
Diodon liturosus

Elongated oval body, almost circular crossways. Snout is blunt and slightly concave near the eyes. Its sturdy dental plates are used to crack the armor of crustaceans and the shells of mollusks. Body is adorned with large dark spots edged in white. The spines on its body and head are mobile. During the day it tends to stay hidden in grottos and areas with little illumination. Up to 65 centimeters long.

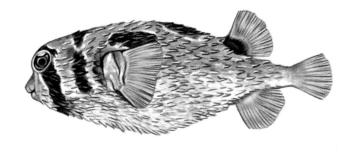

168 Sea turtles are quite common in Malaysia. This one seems to be posing for the camera.

Cover
The image depicts a giant gorgonian (Subergorgia sp.).

Back cover - top
The vivid red of a Gorgonian sea whip (Lophogorgia sp.) enlights the blue depths.

Back cover - bottom
A group of jacks (Caranx sexfasciatus) swims in front of the photographer.

The author would like to thank:
Vanna Cammelli and the staff of Aquadiving Tours, Ron Holland, Clement Lee, Randy Davis and the staff of Borneo Divers, Robert and the staff of the Sipadan Mabu Resort - Smart, the staff of the Layang Island Resort Cressi Sub, Malaysian Airlines Hugyfot, Fraco Sub - Sea & Sea

All photographs are by Andrea and Antonella Ferrari
The photographs of wrecks are by Michael Aw/Borneo Divers